Writing the Critical Essay

ENERGY ALTERNATIVES

An OPPOSING VIEWPOINTS® Guide

Lauri S. Friedman, *Book Editor*

Bruce Glassman, *Vice President*
Bonnie Szumski, *Publisher, Series Editor*
Helen Cothran, *Managing Editor*

OPPOSING
VIEWPOINTS®
SERIES

GREENHAVEN PRESS
An imprint of Thomson Gale, a part of The Thomson Corporation

THOMSON
———— ✦ ————
GALE

Detroit • New York • San Francisco • San Diego • New Haven, Conn. • Waterville, Maine • London • Munich

© 2006 Thomson Gale, a part of The Thomson Corporation.

Thomson and Star Logo are trademarks and Gale and Greenhaven Press are registered trademarks used herein under license.

For more information, contact
Greenhaven Press
27500 Drake Rd.
Farmington Hills, MI 48331-3535
Or you can visit our Internet site at http://www.gale.com

Every effort has been made to trace the owners of copyrighted material.

LIBRARY OF CONGRESS CATALOGING-IN-PUBLICATION DATA

Energy alternatives / Lauri S. Friedman, book editor.
   p. cm. — (Writing the critical essay)

urces. 3. Essay—Authorship. 4. Rhetoric.

2005042445

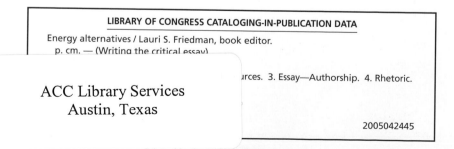
Printed in the United States of America

CONTENTS

Section Two: Model Essays and Writing Exercises

Section Three: Supporting Research Material

Examining the state of writing and how it is taught in the United States was the official purpose of the National Commission on Writing in America's Schools and Colleges. The commission, made up of teachers, school administrators, business leaders, and college and university presidents, released its first report in 2003. "Despite the best efforts of many educators," commissioners argued, "writing has not received the full attention it deserves." Among the findings of the commission was that most fourth-grade students spent less than three hours a week writing, that three-quarters of high school seniors never receive a writing assignment in their history or social studies classes, and that more than 50 percent of first-year students in college have problems writing error-free papers. The commission called for a "cultural sea change" that would increase the emphasis on writing for both elementary and secondary schools. These conclusions have made some educators realize that writing must be emphasized in the curriculum. As colleges are demanding an ever-higher level of writing proficiency from incoming students, schools must respond by making students more competent writers. In response to these concerns, the SAT, an influential standardized test used for college admissions, required an essay for the first time in 2005.

Books in the Writing the Critical Essay: An Opposing Viewpoints Guide series use the patented Opposing Viewpoints format to help students learn to organize ideas and arguments and to write essays using common critical writing techniques. Each book in the series focuses on a particular type of essay writing—including expository, persuasive, descriptive, and narrative—that students learn while being taught both the five-paragraph essay as well as longer pieces of writing that have an opinionated focus. These guides include everything necessary to help students research, outline, draft, edit, and ultimately write successful essays across the curriculum, including essays for the SAT.

Using Opposing Viewpoints

This series is inspired by and builds upon Greenhaven Press's acclaimed Opposing Viewpoints series. As in the parent series, each book in the Writing the Critical Essay series focuses on a timely and controversial social issue that provides lots of opportunities for creating thought-provoking essays. The first section of each volume begins with a brief introductory essay that provides context for the opposing viewpoints that follow. These articles are chosen for their accessibility and clearly stated views. The thesis of each article is made explicit in the article's title and is accentuated by its pairing with an opposing or alternative view. These essays are both models of persuasive writing techniques and valuable research material that students can mine to write their own informed essays. Guided reading and discussion questions help lead students to key ideas and writing techniques presented in the selections.

The second section of each book begins with a preface discussing the format of the essays and examining characteristics of the featured essay type. Model five-paragraph and longer essays then demonstrate that essay type. The essays are annotated so that key writing elements and techniques are pointed out to the student. Sequential, step-by-step exercises help students construct and refine thesis statements; organize material into outlines; analyze and try out writing techniques; write transitions, introductions, and conclusions; and incorporate quotations and other researched material. Ultimately, students construct their own compositions using the designated essay type.

The third section of each volume provides additional research material and writing prompts to help the student. Additional facts about the topic of the book serve as a convenient source of supporting material for essays. Other features help students go beyond the book for their research. Like other Greenhaven Press books, each book in the Writing the Critical Essay series includes bibliographic listings of relevant periodical articles, books, Web sites, and organizations to contact.

Writing the Critical Essay: An Opposing Viewpoints Guide will help students master essay techniques that can be used in any discipline.

Background to Controversy: Why Consider Energy Alternatives?

In the time since oil production began nearly two centuries ago, it has become the lifeblood of global society. It is the force behind the world's transportation systems. It is also the source from which indispensable modern products, such as plastic, are made. For these reasons, oil has been hailed by the U.S. State Department as "the greatest material prize in world history" and is commonly referred to as "black gold" because of the vast fortunes it can yield. On the other hand, oil carries with it heavy environmental, social, and political costs. Wars have been fought in its name and vast ecosystems scarred in its pursuit. This legacy has caused its use to be lamented by some, such as former Venezuelan oil minister Juan Pablo Perez Alfonzo, who once referred to oil as "the excrement of the devil."

Reasons to Consider Energy Alternatives

As more corners of the world become incorporated into the fossil-fuel economy, problems with using oil become more apparent. Today people engage in heated debates over whether oil should be replaced with other types of energy sources and what types of energy alternatives are most efficient. Chief among these issues is how much oil actually remains on the planet. Some contend that energy alternatives are necessary because the world is running out of oil. Some analysts contend the peak will be within five or ten years; more conservative estimates put the range closer to thirty, sixty, or even ninety years. However, with every passing year nations such as China and India are rapidly modernizing, adding to the global

7

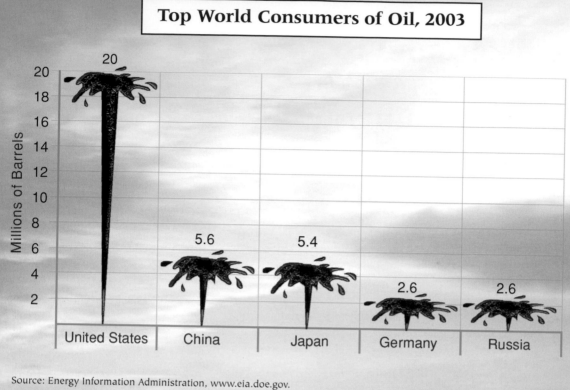

Top World Consumers of Oil, 2003

Millions of Barrels

United States	20
China	5.6
Japan	5.4
Germany	2.6
Russia	2.6

Source: Energy Information Administration, www.eia.doe.gov.

rate of fossil-fuel consumption—the Energy Information Administration expects that by 2025 the world will consume 121 million barrels per day. With such high consumption rates, it is difficult to say how long supplies will last or if they will continue to be affordable to extract. Therefore, pinpointing a year that oil will begin to decline seems less important than acknowledging that sometime in the relatively near future—whether it be ten years or even one hundred years—the sun will likely set on the planet's attainable supply of fossil fuels.

Like supply, environmental concerns have long been a reason to consider energy alternatives. When fossil fuels such as coal or oil are burned, they produce carbon dioxide, which collects in the earth's atmosphere. Too much carbon dioxide can lead to a condition known as global warming, which could have catastrophic effects. Furthermore, the burning of fossil fuels creates air pollution, water pollution, acid rain, and a host of other conditions. Authors Kim Carlyle and Sandra Lewis have described the environmental costs of using oil: "To discover and recover oil, roads are slashed through rainforests, drilling sites contaminate fresh water and soil, leaky pipelines spill millions of gallons of crude oil on wildlife and pristine tundra. . . . The true costs of fossil fuels are staggering and cannot be measured in dollars alone." Many people, therefore, want to investigate

The United States remains dependent on fossil fuels, including gasoline, as the principal source of its energy needs.

energy alternatives in order to slow or reverse the environmental damage caused by fossil fuels.

One of the most persuasive arguments frequently posited for employing energy alternatives is also the most recent: Fossil-fuel consumption puts the United States in dangerous and costly international situations and makes it vulnerable to terrorism. Indeed, over the last thirty years ensuring access to oil has caused the United States to get increasingly involved in the affairs of the Middle East, which is home to about 65 percent of the world's oil. As late-night comedian Jay Leno once aptly put it, the United States never would have gotten involved in the 1991 Gulf War to liberate the nation of Kuwait from an Iraqi invasion had Kuwait's main export been broccoli. Many observers believe the 2003 war in Iraq was also undertaken in part to protect the United States's access to oil. This possibility was not lost on the enemies of the United States and its allies. In fact, when the anti-American insurgency began resisting the American occupation, its first targets were oil pipelines and refineries around Iraq.

Alternatives to Fossil Fuels

When people discuss energy alternatives, they usually mean non-fossil-fuel–based energies. But *energy alternatives* is a broad name for an entire class of very different kinds of energy sources, all of which have distinct advantages and disadvantages. Although all of them have the capability to produce usable energy, no one source is without issue. Chief among these energy alternatives is nuclear power. Nuclear power can provide enormous quantities of energy using very little raw material and without causing air pollution or contributing to global warming; it already provides about 20 percent of the energy America consumes. Yet controversy swirls around whether it causes cancer and other diseases, whether its waste products are safely containable, and, most frightening, whether nuclear power plants could be vulnerable to terrorist

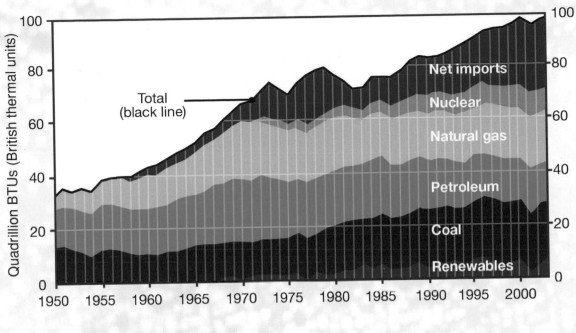

U.S. Sources of Energy

Y-axis: Quadrillion BTUs (British thermal units)

Total (black line)

Net imports
Nuclear
Natural gas
Petroleum
Coal
Renewables

1950 1955 1960 1965 1970 1975 1980 1985 1990 1995 2000

Source: *Weekly Standard*, September 29, 2003.

attack, which would create horrific damage on an almost unimaginable scale.

Other energy alternatives come from renewable sources of power, such as sunlight or wind. The popularity of these energy alternatives is increasing since they provide safe, pollution-free power that can be generated on American soil. Yet solar and wind power have trouble generating large enough quantities of power to sustain widespread energy needs, and the equipment necessary to generate these power sources also must occupy large spaces of land and animal habitat to do so. These drawbacks have in part prevented them from becoming more widely used.

Another alternative energy source is biomass fuel. Biomass energy comes from burnt animal and plant matter. Advocates of this energy source say that harvesting carefully replenished crops and forests, or animal waste such as dung, can yield a high-energy fuel at a low cost to the environment. Like other renewable resources, however, it can be difficult to make biomass fuel work. For example, ethanol, an alcohol made from corn, can already power many of today's automobiles. But planting, growing, and harvesting enough corn to make fuel for the majority of America's cars is a significant obstacle to effectively using this energy source. However, specialized, genetically engineered crops of corn may be grown in the future, which might help biomass become a more effective and cost-efficient energy alternative.

Hydrogen is another emerging alternative energy source. Hydrogen burns cleanly, is abundant on Earth, and, when properly processed, can make an extremely efficient fuel source for transportation vehicles. If hydrogen technology is perfected, it could completely revolutionize America's auto industry. According to author Matt Biven, "No less a person than Henry Ford's great-grandson, Ford Motor chairman William Ford, says hydrogen will put an end to 'the 100-year reign of the internal-combustion engine.'" Yet current hydrogen technology is very limited, and harvesting hydrogen for power can actually require large amounts of fossil fuels, which reduces its usefulness as an energy alternative.

In the end, it is likely that the United States, and the world, will come not to depend on just one energy source but on a combination of sources. Relying on a mix of energy sources could be the best way to ensure economic efficiency, environmental health, political stability, and long-term usage. As the following essays show, the ever-developing debates over energy alternatives are as varied and colorful as the proposed solutions themselves. The sample essays in Section One provide a sampling of some of the key dialogues regarding energy alternatives.

Section One:
Opposing
Viewpoints
on Energy
Alternatives

It Is Necessary to Find Alternative Energy Sources

Tim Appenzeller

In the following essay, Tim Appenzeller argues that the end of the oil era is fast approaching. He discusses the estimates of experts who agree that in a relatively short amount of time the world's oil reserves will begin drying up and oil will become dramatically more expensive. Because nearly every product in American society is connected in some way to petroleum, this will have drastic economic, political, and environmental consequences on the United States and on the global economy. Therefore, the author concludes that the United States should wean itself off oil and find alternative energy sources to power its expanding economy. Journalist Tim Appenzeller is an editor at *U.S. News & World Report*.

Consider the following questions:

1. How much of the world's oil does America consume?
2. Why does the author believe the "quest for oil is a losing game"?
3. In what year do some oil experts expect the world oil supply to peak?

You wouldn't know it from the hulking SUVs [sport utility vehicles] and traffic-clogged freeways of the United States, but we're in the twilight of plentiful oil. There's no global shortage yet; far from it. The world can still produce so much crude that the current price of about $30 for a

Tim Appenzeller, "The End of Cheap Oil," *National Geographic*, vol. 205, June 2004.
Copyright © 2004 by the National Geographic Society. Reproduced by permission.

42-gallon barrel would plummet if the Organization of the Petroleum Exporting Countries (OPEC) did not limit production. This abundance of oil means, for now, that oil is cheap. In the United States, where gasoline taxes average 43 cents a gallon (instead of dollars, as in Europe and Japan), a gallon of gasoline can be cheaper than a bottle of water—making it too cheap for most people to bother conserving. While oil demand is up everywhere, the U.S. remains the king of consumers, slurping up a quarter of the world's oil—about three gallons a person every day—even though it has just 5 percent of the population.

The Twilight of Plentiful Oil

Yet as [many] drillers know, slaking the world's oil thirst is harder than it used to be. The old sources can't be counted on anymore. On land the lower 48 states of the

Despite the problems associated with America's dependence on oil, SUVs such as the Hummer 2, which get very low gasoline mileage, are popular among American drivers.

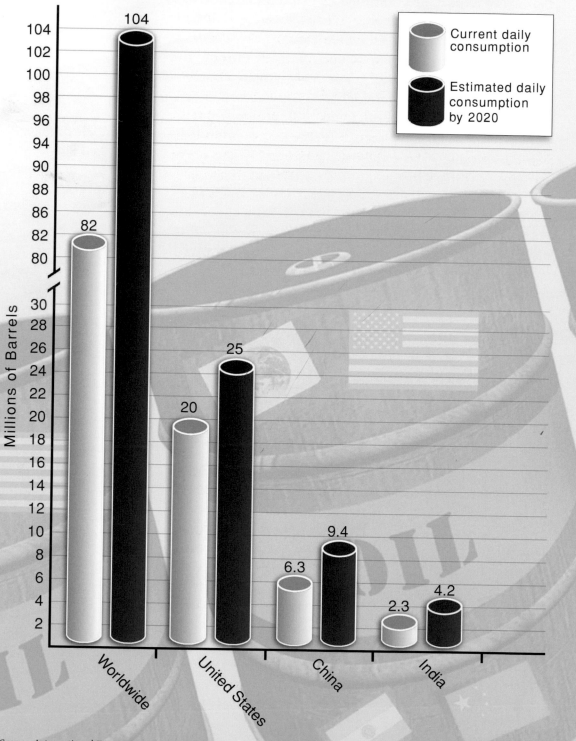

A Growing Problem: Projected Energy Use

Millions of Barrels

Legend:
- Current daily consumption
- Estimated daily consumption by 2020

Worldwide: 82, 104
United States: 20, 25
China: 6.3, 9.4
India: 2.3, 4.2

Source: International Energy Agency, www.iea.org.

U.S. are tapped out, producing less than half the oil they did at their peak in 1970. Production from the North Slope of Alaska and the North Sea of Europe, burgeoning oil regions 20 years ago, is in decline. Unrest in Venezuela and Nigeria threatens the flow of oil. The Middle East remains the mother lode of crude, but war and instability underscore the perils of depending on that region.

And so oil companies are searching for new supplies and braving high costs, both human and economic. Making gambles like . . . venturing into West Africa and Russia, they are still finding oil in quantities to gladden a Hummer owner's heart. But in the end the quest for more cheap oil will prove a losing game: Not just because oil consumption imposes severe costs on the environment, health, and taxpayers, but also because the world's oil addiction is hastening a day of reckoning.

A Collision Course with Geology

Humanity's way of life is on a collision course with geology—with the stark fact that the Earth holds a finite supply of oil. The flood of crude from fields around the world will ultimately top out, then dwindle. It could be 5 years from now or 30: No one knows for sure, and geologists and economists are embroiled in debate about just when the "oil peak" will be upon us. But few doubt that it is coming. "In our lifetime," says economist Robert K. Kaufmann of Boston University, who is 46, "we will have to deal with a peak in the supply of cheap oil."

The peak will be a watershed moment, marking the change from an increasing supply of cheap oil to a dwindling supply of expensive oil. Some experts foresee dire consequences: shortages, price spikes, economic disruption, and a desperate push to wrest oil from "unconventional" sources such as tar sands, oil shale, or coal. Others think that by curbing our oil use and developing sustainable alternatives now, we can delay the peak and wean ourselves more easily when the inevitable happens. "There are many things you can do to ease the transition," says Alfred Cavallo, an energy consultant in Princeton, New Jersey. "And you can have a very nice life on a sustainable system. Of course, not everyone is going to be driving SUVs.". . .

Oil Consumption Is Expected to Grow

The world can now feed a daily oil habit of nearly 80 million barrels. In the U.S. about two-thirds of the oil goes to make fuel for cars, trucks, and planes. But the synthetic fabrics in our wardrobe and the plastics in just about everything we touch started out as oil too. We can also thank oil and its cousin, natural gas, for the cheap and plentiful food at the supermarket, grown with the help of hydrocarbon-based fertilizers and pesticides. As Daniel Yergin writes in his oil history *The Prize*, we live in "the Age of Hydrocarbon Man."

Oil prices hit record highs in 2005, driving prices at the pump to levels never before seen.

Around the world Hydrocarbon Man is getting thirstier. In the U.S., where oil consumption is expected to grow nearly 50 percent in 20 years, carmakers are touting horsepower as they did in the muscle-car 1960s. SUVs and minivans are displacing thriftier sedans and wagons

as the standard family car. Even the tax code encourages consumption, offering people who buy the biggest SUVs for business use a deduction of up to $100,000. Since 1988 the average gas mileage of U.S. passenger vehicles has fallen, while the world has burned up more than a third of a trillion barrels of irreplaceable oil. . . .

Some oil wells have experienced a dramatic decline in production, supporting claims that the world is running out of oil.

Sooner or Later, the Oil Will Run Out

These days a raging debate divides oil experts, with prophets of imminent shortage pitted against believers in at least a couple more decades of abundance. Pessimists note that oil prospectors had their best luck in the early 1960s, and that discoveries have slowed since then. They conclude that little conventional oil is left to be found and that the oil peak could be upon us by 2010. . . .

On the optimistic side, the United States Geological Survey (USGS) concluded in a 2000 study that there's at least 50 percent more oil left than the pessimists believe, much of it in the Middle East. New technologies will wring additional supplies from existing fields, the USGS predicts, and vast new reserves remain to be found. Many economists agree, saying discoveries have fallen off simply because countries awash in oil like Iraq, Iran, and Saudi Arabia have had no incentive to drill for more. "If I'm an OPEC producer, with lots of spare capacity, why would I waste money looking for more reserves?" asks Kaufmann.

But in the end, "you're talking about a few years one way or another," says Cavallo, the Princeton consultant. Thomas Ahlbrandt, the geologist who led the USGS study, says that even the larger reserves he envisions can't sustain the world's growing thirst for oil indefinitely. "Oil and gas are limited," he says flatly. "My personal feeling is, we have a concern in the next couple of decades."

Analyze the essay:

1. In the essay you just read, the author uses statements from professionals to make the most direct assertions that the world is running out of oil. Does his use of these statements by experts influence your opinion of the author's essay? Why or why not?

2. Although the author has written an essay that argues the world is running out of oil, he cites a study that found there is at least 50 percent more oil left in the world than some people believe. Why do you think he has included such information? What benefit do you think can be gained from using information in your essay that does not immediately reflect the overall point you are trying to argue?

It Is Not Necessary to Find Alternative Energy Sources

M.A. Adelman

M.A. Adelman is a professor of economics at the Massachusetts Institute of Technology. In the following essay he argues that the idea that the world will someday run out of oil is a myth. He contends that it is impossible to know for sure how much oil the world contains. Oil-producing countries are reluctant to look for new sources—they want to maintain the illusion that supplies are short in order to keep prices high. Furthermore, the author maintains that the world's oil supply is much greater than we can imagine, for oil continues to be found as new technologies are developed to extract it. The author concludes that doomsday theories that call for alternative energy sources are based on misinformation and a concerted effort by oil companies to keep prices high.

Consider the following questions:

1. When does the author believe the world's supply of oil will be exhausted?
2. How much greater was world oil production in 2003 than in the late nineteenth century, according to Adelman?
3. According to the author, why doesn't Saudi Arabia actively work to discover and develop more oil fields?

According to "conventional wisdom," humanity's need for oil cannot be met and a gap will soon emerge between demand and supply. That gap will broaden as

M.A. Adelman, "The Real Oil Problem," *Regulation*, Spring 2004. Copyright © 2004 by the Cato Institute. All rights reserved. Reproduced by permission.

In 1875 geologist John Strong Newberry warned that the world's oil supply was in danger of running out.

the economies of Europe, Japan, and several emerging nations grow and increase their energy needs. The United States is at the mercy of Middle Eastern exporters who can use the "oil weapon" to cripple the U.S. economy. Unless we increase domestic oil production radically or cut consumption, or nations like Russia quickly exploit recently discovered oil fields, the United States will find itself in an oil crisis.

But conventional wisdom "knows" many things that are not true. There is not, and never has been, an oil crisis or gap. Oil reserves are not dwindling. . . .

Oil Myths

In 1875, John Strong Newberry, the chief geologist of the state of Ohio, predicted that the supply of oil would soon run out. The alarm has been sounded repeatedly in the many decades since. In 1973, State Department analyst James Akins, then the chief U.S. policymaker on oil, published "The Oil Crisis: This time the wolf is here," in which he called for more domestic production and for improved relations with oil-producing nations in the Middle East. In 1979, President Jimmy Carter, echoing a CIA assessment, said that oil wells "were drying up all over the world." Just last year [in 2003], the *New York Times* reported that "oil reserves are expected to dwindle in the decades ahead," while the International Energy Agency forecasted that oil output will grow in the Persian Gulf between now and 2030, but it will decline elsewhere.

The doomsday predictions have all proved false. In 2003, world oil production was 4,400 times greater than it was in Newberry's day, but the price per unit was probably lower. Oil reserves and production even outside the Middle East are greater today than they were when Akins claimed the wolf was here. World output of oil is up a quarter since Carter's "drying up" pronouncement, but Middle East exports peaked in 1976–77.

Despite all those facts, the predictions of doom keep on coming. . . .

It is commonly asked, when will the world's supply of oil be exhausted? The best one-word answer: Never. Since the human race began to use minerals, there has been eternal struggle—stingy nature versus inquisitive mankind. The payoff is the price of the mineral, and mankind has won big, so far.

However, alarmists point to world oil prices and claim that what has happened "so far" will not continue much longer. They might have a point—if the world oil market featured several different, competitive suppliers. But instead, it is dominated by a monopoly supplier, so the higher prices in themselves mean nothing. To understand this, one needs a quick course in resource economics.

Minerals are produced from reserves, which are mineral deposits discovered and identified as able to be extracted profitably. Are oil reserves dwindling? Is it getting harder to

We Are Not Running Out of Oil

Probable resources of oil, gas, and coal are officially forecast to be 114, 200, and 1,884 years of present usage, respectively.

Robert L. Bradley Jr., "The Growing Abundance of Fossil Fuels," *Freeman: Ideas on Liberty*, November 1999.

find or create them? Conventional wisdom says: Of course. But once again, conventional wisdom is wrong. . . .

The dwindling of reserves is a legend firmly believed because it seems so obvious. Assume any number for the size of reserves. From it, subtract a few years' current output. The conclusion is absolutely sure: Reserves are dwindling; the wolf is getting closer. In time, production must cease. Oil in the ground becomes constantly more valuable—so much so that a gap forms between how much oil we want and how much we are able to afford because of scarcity. Civilization cannot continue without oil, so something must be done.

The Myth of Scarcity Keeps Prices High

Politics and economics have a large impact on how much oil is produced in OPEC countries such as Iraq, where this oil refinery is located.

And indeed, in some times and places the oil does run down. Output in the Appalachian United States had peaked by 1900, and output in Texas peaked in 1972. But the "running out" vision never works globally. At the end of 1970, non-OPEC [Organization of Petroleum Exporting Countries] countries had about 200 billion remaining in

proved reserves. In the next 33 years, those countries produced 460 billion barrels and now have 209 billion "remaining." The producers kept using up their inventory, at a rate of about seven percent per year, and then replacing it. The OPEC countries started with about 412 billion in proved reserves, produced 307 billion, and now have about 819 billion left. Their reserve numbers are shaky, but clearly they had—and have—a lot more inventory than they used up. Saudi Arabia alone has over 80 known fields and exploits only nine. Of course, there are many more fields, known and unknown. The Saudis do not invest to discover, develop, and produce more oil because more production would bring down world prices.

Growing knowledge lowers cost, unlocks new deposits in existing areas, and opens new areas for discovery. In 1950, there was no offshore oil production; it was highly "unconventional" oil. Some 25 years later, offshore wells were being drilled in water 1,000 feet deep. And 25 years

Deep-water drilling allows drillers to tap oil deposits found deep in the ocean floor, adding to the global supply.

after that, oilmen were drilling in water 10,000 feet deep—once technological advancement enabled them to drill without the costly steel structure that had earlier made deep-water drilling too expensive. Today, a third of all U.S. oil production comes from offshore wells. Given current knowledge and technique, the U.S. Geological Survey predicts offshore oil will ultimately comprise 50 percent of U.S. production. . . .

Oil Estimates Are Meaningless or Wrong

To sum up: There is no indication that non-OPEC oil is getting more expensive to find and develop. Statements about non-OPEC nations' "dwindling reserves" are meaningless or wrong. . . .

U.S. oil policies are based on fantasies not facts: gaps, shortages, and surpluses. Those ideas are at the core of the Carter legislation, and of the current Energy Bill. The Carter White House also believed what the current [George W.] Bush White House believes—that, in the face of all evidence, they are getting binding assurance of supply by OPEC, or by Saudi Arabia. That myth is part of the larger myth that the world is running out of oil.

Analyze the essay:

1. Adelman writes of the power of "conventional wisdom," which refers to a belief or idea that is commonly held by the general public—in this case, the notion that the world is running out of oil. In your opinion, does Adelman's essay successfully debunk conventional wisdom? Why or why not?

2. In this viewpoint, the author argues that the world is not running out of oil; he counters the opinion of the previous author, who believes the world is running out of oil. After reading both viewpoints, which do you find more persuasive? Why? Can you identify a particular technique or argument that helped sway you?

Renewable Resources Can Be a Practical Source of Energy

Alan Reder

In the following essay freelance writer Alan Reder argues that renewable resources are a viable energy source. He focuses on the case of Bob Maynard, an Oregon man whose suburban home is equipped with solar panels that provide enough energy to power modern appliances such as computers, televisions, refrigerators, and washing machines. Moreover, this energy is nonpolluting and cost efficient: When the Maynards produce more energy than they need, they accrue energy credits that can be used when they are unable to draw energy directly from the sun.

Consider the following questions:

1. Which states offer rebates of 50 and 70 percent to homeowners who purchase solar energy systems?
2. How much did utility costs increase in 2003?

Not very long ago, owning a solar-powered home branded folks the way, say, wearing dreadlocks did. You could guess with reasonable accuracy their favorite band (Grateful Dead), what they'd eaten for lunch (veggie burger), and where they resided (miles from Main Street, both physically and mentally). . . .

But, oh, how times have changed. McDonald's is now test-marketing veggie burgers, and the solar dudes are moving to the suburbs. Take Bob Maynard.

A growing number of American homes are powered by solar energy, captured by solar panels placed on rooftops.

"The World . . . Is Catching Up"

Ten years ago, Maynard was living a fair distance from the world of cul-de-sacs and Cuisinarts. He and his first wife lived in a small solar-powered cabin in southern Oregon's rural Illinois Valley. They produced all their own electricity, and while this had certain psychological benefits (a pioneer's sense of self-reliance and freedom), it also had its drawbacks (fewer—and smaller—appliances than you'd find in many studio apartments).

But after a decade of rural exile, Maynard now lives with his second wife, Barb, in a three-bedroom, two-bath ranch-style house in suburban Grants Pass, Oregon. Both inside and out, the Maynards' place doesn't look much different from their neighbors'. They own two computers, two aquariums, a 21-cubic-foot Amana fridge, a full-size washer and dryer, and an entertainment center complete with tower speakers and a large-screen TV, and they use all of it as much as they want.

It would seem that Bob had gone from being a classic eco-freak to a classic sellout. But he hasn't given up his photovoltaic panels [that capture energy from the sun] any more than he's abandoned his environmental leanings. It's just that the world finally is catching up with Bob Maynard.

Renewable Resources Can Run Entire Homes

Without much fanfare, solar power has blossomed into a viable option for conventional householders—i.e., suburbanites. Early on, when people like the Maynards chose to go solar, they did so at a cost that few middle-class Americans would tolerate. Back in their old cabin, the Maynards watched TV on a paltry 13-inch set and listened to music on a tinny boom box, because brawnier gear sucked more power than their system could provide. For the same reason, they cooled their food in a modest 16-cubic-foot Sun Frost refrigerator, which offered unmatched

Modern solar technology is capable of generating enough electricity to meet most of the energy needs of the typical American home.

energy efficiency but a steep price tag of $2,500. And forget running a load of laundry after dinner: Once the sun went down, the system ran entirely on stored power from backup batteries, and that supply was mercilessly finite.

Today the Maynards can run their appliances as much as they want to because they get backup electricity from the same place their neighbors do: Pacific Power, their local utility. Whenever their home's electric load becomes too much for the system, it automatically draws power from the utility grid. The beauty is, the Maynards still get most of their juice from the sky (except during those sun-starved months of winter) via a 3.3-kilowatt solar energy system, whose photovoltaic panels lie flat against a mere 250 square feet of their roof. Last summer [2003], the Maynards' system actually generated more power than they used, and according to the neat digital readout in their garage, the system has actually prevented more than 2,180 pounds of carbon pollution from entering the air since the Maynards installed it in May [2003]. (By contrast, the average home's use of conventional electricity is responsible for 22,000 pounds of carbon pollution annually, according to the Environmental Protection Agency.) Combine that with falling prices for home solar

Solar-powered homes can draw backup power from local utility grids whenever energy needs exceed the capacity of the home system.

systems (seven-fold In the past two decades) and rising utility costs (up six percent nationwide [in 2003] alone), and suddenly solar seems like a bright idea. . . .

Credits, Rebates, and Savings Make Solar Power Affordable

But a complete home system doesn't come cheap. Most systems cost in the neighborhood of a decent new car, though the incentives to buy are often a lot better than the ones at your local dealership. At present, every state but South Carolina offers some combination of tax credits, rebates, and other financial enticements to encourage home-owners to go solar. The Maynards' home state of Oregon offers one of the best incentive packages around, but some other states offer programs that match or beat it. New Jersey currently rebates up to 70 percent of a system's total cost, and California pays back up to 50 percent, notes Richard Perez, co-publisher of *Home Power* magazine.

When you take into account the rebates and other incentives, plus the cost of conventional electricity, most solar systems pay for themselves within 15 years (although

Each home that runs on conventional electricity is responsible for about 22,000 pounds of carbon pollution released into the atmosphere each year.

in areas without good sunlight, it can take longer). But in certain parts of the country, solar power can work to your economic advantage much sooner. In parts of sunny California, electricity rates vary according to the time of day, with some utility customers paying a whopping 35 cents per kilowatt hour in the afternoon, when demand for power is greatest. That's also when photovoltaic productivity peaks, so most grid-tied systems feed power back to the grid at that time, with their owners earning credits (rather than paying for juice) at the 35-cent rate. Those ratepayers might actually break even—or better—with a grid-tied system. . . .

And consider this: During the next blackout, you'll probably still be surfing the Web and watching *Survivor* while your neighbors stumble around in the dark.

Analyze the essay:

1. In this essay Alan Reder discusses how many states provide financial incentives such as rebates or tax credits to encourage or reward citizens for using renewable power sources. In the following viewpoint, the editors of the *Colorado Springs Gazette* argue that the government should not be in the business of financially subsidizing alternative energy sources. After reading both essays, which viewpoint do you find more persuasive? Why?

2. Reder focuses on the case of Bob Maynard to illustrate his point about solar power. In your opinion, does the experience of one person provide enough evidence to prove that renewable resources can replace traditional power on a widespread scale? Why or why not?

Renewable Resources Are Not Practical Energy Sources

Colorado Springs Gazette

The following editorial published in the *Colorado Springs Gazette* argues that renewable resources are impractical energy sources that cannot meaningfully contribute to America's energy supply. The editors contend that although they do not produce pollution in the same way as traditional energy sources, renewables have negative trade-offs, such as high cost, inefficiency, and their effect on the environment. Finally, the editors argue that if renewable resources were truly viable, they would be flourishing and they would not need to be kept alive by government subsidies.

Consider the following questions:

1. What similarities do the editors see between the story of Don Quixote and proponents of renewable resources?
2. Why do the editors believe that it is wrong for the government to subsidize renewable resources?
3. What is the drawback of a battery-powered car, according to the *Gazette*?

Don Quixote tilting at windmills makes a wonderfully romantic image. In a shaving basin, [author Miguel de] Cervantes' hero found a magic helmet; in the tramp Aldonza he saw the beautiful and unblemished Dulcinea. But the old man was, we know, deluded. And it's this same strain of delusion that fuels the Quixotic

Large areas of outdoor space are needed to erect the number of windmills required to generate electricity.

quest to turn a petroleum-based economy into one powered by windmills, moon beams, gerbil wheels and other alternative energy panaceas.

Alternative energy enthusiasts aren't bad people, but they frequently are tilting at windmills [that is, chasing impossible goals]. Their futuristic fantasies are harmless enough when kept to themselves. But danger arises when they succeed in dragooning governments and taxpayers into mandating or subsidizing their flights of fancy, as they are trying to do in pressuring Colorado Springs Utilities to abandon a planned coal-fired power plant in favor of wind farms and conservation.

Renewable Resources Damage in Their Own Way

Could wind power someday have a place in the city's energy portfolio? Possibly, when the technology, times and economics make market sense. Will wind farms any time soon be able to supplant a traditional power plant in delivering the most energy bang for the buck? That's unlikely, unless advocates intend that we pave all of eastern El Paso County with windmills and solar panels.

Because contrary to a related delusion, this is not a trade-off-free world. And what trade-offs are renewable energy enthusiasts really willing to make? Traditional power plants pollute (though we've made great strides in reducing emissions and will likely make more), but they leave a relatively small "footprint" on the land. The same can't be said for the kinds of wind farms we'd need to put a dent in a growing city's future energy demands.

A worker helps to erect a wind turbine in Texas. Such turbines work by converting the kinetic power of wind into electricity.

How many thousands of acres of beloved "open spaces" are windmill farm backers willing to obliterate along the way? How many precious "view corridors" will be ruined? How much endangered species habitat consumed? The impacts upon allegedly endangered Preble's meadow jumping mice could be catastrophic; and how many fluffy little mountain plovers [a type of bird] are we willing to sacrifice annually to those whirling turbine blades?

Renewables Are Unable to Meet Power Demand

In case some in the community haven't noticed, we live in a petroleum-based society, and rely on fossil fuels—oil, coal, natural gas, among them—not just to move our cars and heat our homes but to manufacture and grow and transport virtually everything we use or consume. A failure to recognize and accept this fundamental reality, as well as the fact that it's not likely to change dramatically in the near term, at least without turning this society on its head, is the first step down the path to their Quixotic other world.

It's true we should conserve more, based on voluntary actions spurred by education and economic and market incentives. And it's probable that windmills, solar panels, biomass and other alternative energy sources may in time play a greater part in America's energy portfolio. But if such alternative approaches are as viable as proponents say they are, they wouldn't have to seek government subsidies and mandates in order to force them into being.

The free enterprise system is amazingly quick and efficient, even relentless, in finding applications for virtually any technology and innovation that spring to mind. So why hasn't it done so when it comes to so many alter-

> ### Paving Nature
>
> To produce the . . . electricity America will need by 2010, using only wind or solar power, we would have to blanket 9,400,000 acres with windmills or solar panels . . . an area equal to Connecticut, Delaware, and Massachusetts combined!
>
> Paul K. Driessen, "The False Promise of Renewable Energy," www.heartland.org, May 2001.

native energy panaceas? Because those technologies have costs, trade-offs and limitations that make them less viable than existing alternatives.

Pie in the Sky

Battery powered cars reduce gasoline consumption. But when you plug one in at home for a recharge, where is that electricity coming from? A coal or natural gas-fired power plant, most likely. So are you really saving resources and cutting air pollution when you drive a battery powered car, or just imagining that you are?

The fact is, in terms of cost, efficiency, reliability and bang for the buck, fossil fuels simply can't be beaten at

A technician performs maintenance at a natural gas plant. A gaseous fossil fuel, natural gas is burned to generate electricity in power plants across the United States.

this point in time. We're not arguing that alternatives could never become economically viable—just that the markets and private initiative should determine that, as opposed to the creation of false markets via government subsidies and mandates. When these technologies become profitable, affordable and reliable enough to raise a glitter in the venture capitalist's eye (as opposed to subsidy-chasers), interests will step forward to make it happen. But until then, we would be prudent to choose the tried and true over the pie in the sky.

Analyze the essay:

1. In the essay you just read, the editors argue that wind farms and solar panels are bad for the environment because they take up lots of land and displace or harm wildlife. Traditional power plants take up much less space than wind farms or solar panels, but they create air pollution, which harms the environment. In your opinion, which energy source damages the environment more seriously? Should this be taken into consideration when deciding which energy source should be pursued?

2. The essay you just read compared renewable resources to "moon beams" and "gerbil wheels." How does framing the issue in this way help support the essay's argument that renewable resources are not an ideal energy source? Do you think this is an effective comparison? Why or why not?

Nuclear Power Is a Viable Alternative Energy Source

Peter W. Huber and Mark P. Mills

Peter W. Huber and Mark P. Mills are cofounders of Digital Power Capital, a group that invests in power technologies. They write frequently about energy policy and the environment; their most recent book is *The Bottomless Well: The Twilight of Fuel, the Virtue of Waste, and Why We Will Never Run Out of Energy*. In the following essay, Huber and Mills argue that nuclear power is a clean, plentiful, and safe power source that is capable of satisfying America's mounting energy needs.

Consider the following questions:

1. According to the authors, what effect did the Three Mile Island accident have on America's view of nuclear power?
2. According to Huber and Mills, how do energy pundits at the *New York Times* and Greenpeace propose to solve the impending energy crisis?
3. How do the authors suggest making nuclear power plants safe from terrorist attacks?

The stunning thing about nuclear power [is that] tiny quantities of raw material can do so much. A bundle of enriched-uranium fuel-rods that could fit into a two-bedroom apartment in Hell's Kitchen [a neighborhood in New York City] would power the city for a year: furnaces, espresso machines, subways, streetlights, stock tickers, Times Square, everything—even our cars and taxis, if we could conveniently plug them into the grid. True, you don't want to stack fuel rods in midtown Manhattan; you don't in fact want to stack them casually on top of one another anywhere. But in suitable reactors, situated, say, 50 miles from the city on a few hundred acres of suitably fortified and well-guarded real estate, two rooms' worth of fuel could electrify it all. . . .

Moving Beyond Our Nuclear Past

For such a nuclear-powered future to arrive, however, we'll need to get beyond our nuclear-power past. In the now-standard histories, the beginning of the end of nuclear power arrived on March 28, 1979, with the meltdown of the uranium core at Three Mile Island in Pennsylvania. The Chernobyl disaster [in the former Soviet Union] seven years later drove the final nail into the nuclear coffin. It didn't matter that the Three Mile Island containment vessel had done its job and prevented any significant release of radioactivity, or that Soviet reactors operated within a system that couldn't build a safe toaster oven. Uranium was finished. . . .

In the ensuing decades, however, American oil consumption rose 15 percent and electricity use almost dou-

Times Square and other parts of New York City consume large amounts of power.

bled. Many people aren't happy about it. Protecting our oil-supply lines entangles us with feudal theocracies and the fanatical sects that they spawn. The coal that we burn to generate so much of our electricity pollutes the air and may warm the planet. What to do? All sober and thoughtful energy pundits at the *New York Times*, Greenpeace, and the Harvard Divinity School agree: the answer to both problems is . . . efficiency and the development of renewable sources of power. Nevertheless, the secretary of energy, his boss (now a Texas oilman, not a Georgia peanut farmer), and the rest of the country should look elsewhere. . . .

When the nuclear power plant on Three Mile Island experienced a meltdown in 1979, safety measures prevented any significant release of radioactivity.

[To] hydrogen, the most optimistic Green visionaries reply—produced by solar cells or windmills. But it's not possible to take such proposals seriously. New York City consumes so much energy that you'd need, at a minimum, to cover two cities with solar cells to power a single city. No conceivable mix of solar and wind could come close to supplying the trillions of additional kilowatt-hours of power we'll soon need.

Nuclear Power: Efficient, Abundant, and Safe

Nuclear power could do it—easily. In all key technical respects, it is the antithesis of solar power. A quad's worth of solar-powered wood is a huge forest—beautiful to behold, but bulky and heavy. Pound for pound, coal stores about twice as much heat. Oil beats coal by about twice as much again. And an ounce of enriched-uranium fuel equals about 4 tons of coal, or 15 barrels of oil. That's why minuscule quantities contained in relatively tiny reactors can power a metropolis.

What's more, North America has vast deposits of uranium ore, and scooping it up is no real challenge. Enrichment accounts for about half of the fuel's cost, and enrichment technologies keep improving. . . .

How worried should we really be in 2005 that accidents or attacks might release and disperse a nuclear power plant's radioactive fuel? Not very. Our civilian nuclear industry has dramatically improved its procedures and safety-related hardware since 1979. Several thousand reactor-years of statistics since Three Mile Island clearly show that these power plants are extraordinarily reliable in normal operation.

And uranium's combination of power and super-density makes the fuel less of a terror risk, not more, at least from an engineering standpoint. It's easy to "overbuild" the protective walls and containment systems of nuclear facilities, since—like the pyramids—the payload they're built to shield is so small. Protecting skyscrapers is hard; no builder can afford to erect a hundred times more wall than usable space. Guaranteeing the integrity of a jumbo jet's fuel tanks is impossible; the tanks have to fly. Shielding a nuclear plant's tiny payload is easy— just erect more steel, pour more concrete, and build tougher perimeters. . . .

Greens don't want to hear it, but nuclear power makes the most environmental sense, too. Nuclear wastes pose

> ## Nuclear Power and Safety
>
> Nuclear power plants have better safety performance today than ever, and future generations of reactors will have design modifications that enhance safety even further.
>
> Richard A. Meserve, "Global Warming and Nuclear Power," *Science*, January 23, 2004.

Asay. © 2001 by Creators Syndicate, Inc. Reproduced by permission.

no serious engineering problems. Uranium is such an energy-rich fuel that the actual volume of waste is tiny compared with that of other fuels, and is easily converted from its already-stable ceramic form as a fuel into an even more stable glass-like compound, and just as easily deposited in deep geological formations, themselves stable for tens of millions of years. And what has Green antinuclear activism achieved since the seventies? Not the reduction in demand for energy that it had hoped for but a massive increase in the use of coal, which burns less clean than uranium. . . .

The Power Has to Come from Somewhere

Serious Greens must face reality. Short of some convulsion that drastically shrinks the economy, demand for electricity will go on rising. Total U.S. electricity consumption will increase another 20 to 30 percent, at least, over the next ten years. . . .

Nuclear power plants are capable of generating enormous quantities of energy.

The power has to come from somewhere. Sun and wind will never come close to supplying it. Earnest though they are, the people who argue otherwise are the folks who brought us 400 million extra tons of coal a year. The one practical technology that could decisively shift U.S. carbon emissions in the near term would displace coal with uranium, since uranium burns emission-free. It's time even for Greens to embrace the atom.

Analyze the essay:

1. The authors compare nuclear power to other alternative energy sources such as solar and wind power. What are some of the comparisons they make? How do these comparisons serve to support the authors' view that nuclear power is a viable energy alternative?

2. The authors open their discussion of nuclear power by colorfully describing how many things in New York City could theoretically be run on nuclear power. Does this type of introduction heighten your interest in the essay topic? How does this opening help to illustrate the authors' larger point?

Nuclear Power Is Not a Viable Alternative Energy Source

Erik Assadourian

In the following essay Erik Assadourian argues that nuclear power is not a viable resource because it leaves behind radioactive nuclear waste and could be used as a weapon by terrorists. He compares it to wind and solar power, which he says are cheaper and safer than nuclear power. For security and environmental reasons, the author advises against turning to nuclear power as a way to meet the world's energy needs. Erik Assadourian is a staff researcher at the Worldwatch Institute, a non-profit organization that advocates environmental stability and social justice.

Consider the following questions:

1. What is Yucca Mountain, and why does the author mention it?
2. When does Belgium plan to completely stop using nuclear power, according to Assadourian?
3. According to the author, how much more expensive is nuclear power than wind power?

A hundred millennia from now, perhaps a new civilization will have arisen atop the remains of the civilization we now know. And as this new society explores the land and its secrets, at the base of what we call Yucca Mountain, Nevada, it may stumble on artifacts that warn—in as universal a way as was conceivable to the

Erik Assadourian, "The New Clear Threat," *Worldwatch*, vol. 16, May/June 2003.
Copyright © 2003 by the Worldwatch Institute, www.worldwatch.org. Reproduced
by permission.

A train transports nuclear waste from a reprocessing plant to a storage facility. Nuclear waste can be very dangerous if not properly contained.

humans that lived before—that those who find these markers should stay away.

Why? Because under that mountain, there will be some 100,000 tons of still-active nuclear waste sitting in barrels—and by then, even in the absence of any geological upheavals in the intervening thousand centuries, about 1 percent of that lethal material (as now estimated by the U.S. Department of Energy) will have leaked out and may have entered the groundwater, creating a spreading plume of contamination.

Of course, we cannot predict what will happen geologically, biologically, or sociologically in 100,000 years. But atomic waste is collecting at 131 minimally secured sites in the United States—and many others around the world—and the need to contain the threat continues to mount.

Nuclear Materials Pose a Grave Threat

In fact, we are finally coming to realize that securing nuclear waste is an essential step in improving environmental and global security. With the collapse of the Soviet Union, the control mechanisms that regulated its stock-piled nuclear waste and weapons of mass destruction (WMD) have withered. Between the 1.5 metric tons of weapons-grade plutonium that are generated each year by Russian nuclear power plants, the tactical nuclear weapons and radioisotope thermal generators that are easily transportable and poorly secured, and the thousands of underemployed weapons scientists, the threat nuclear materials pose to the world's people and environment has become undeniable.

Fortunately, at least in Russia, there is movement to secure WMD and component materials. In 1991, soon after the end of the Cold War, Russia agreed to allow the United States to help secure and decommission part of its arsenal. Under the leadership of U.S. Senators Sam Nunn and Richard Lugar, the Cooperative Threat Reduction program was enacted, and over the course of a decade it has destroyed over 6,000 nuclear warheads, helped to increase security at 40 percent of the facilities housing nuclear materials, and employed tens of thousands of weapons scientists in peaceful pursuits. . . .

We Must End the Nuclear Era

While we may be able to secure these deadly materials in the short run, our civilization is still in its infancy. Governments come and go, empires rise and fall. How can we find a system to contain materials that will last 50 times longer than our recorded history? We don't even have materials that will last this long, except, of course, the ones we're trying to contain. The goal must be to avoid creating any more waste in the first place. Yet how do we do this when 17 percent of the world's electricity comes from nuclear power, using more than 65,000 tons of uranium per year?

Many governments have concluded that, contrary to the claims of nuclear industry advocates, nuclear power is not safe, economical, or pollution-free—and they are starting to phase out this hubristic technology. Belgium, which gets 58 percent of its energy from nuclear power, has introduced legislation that would phase out nuclear power by 2025. Nuclear power plants won't last forever; in the United States their initial licenses are for 40 years. Even with license extensions, if the other 31 nuclear countries were to agree to build no more reactors (and several have agreed already), we could be ushering in a nuclear-free world by mid-century. However, some governments have proposed new construction. In the United States, where no new reactor has been ordered in 25 years, the Energy Department in 2001 released a report promoting the construction of at least one new plant by 2010 and an estimated 50 more by 2020.

Golliver. © 2001 by Gary Oliver. Reproduced by permission.

A Massive Environmental and Security Threat

While proponents of nuclear power argue that it is a cheap and clean alternative to fossil fuels because it does not produce air pollution, nuclear energy is not a viable alternative to renewable energy. Besides creating waste that remains lethal for millennia, nuclear power costs two to three times more than wind power (10–14 cents per kilowatt hour, compared to 4–6 cents). It is also a massive environmental and security threat. In 2002, at the Davis-Besse power plant in Ohio, boric acid ate a hole through the 17-cm thick reactor vessel head. Just half a centimeter of stainless steel prevented the escape of pressurized coolant, which could have triggered a reactor meltdown. In addition, nuclear plants are often unsecured against terrorist attack. In January [2003], 19 Greenpeace activists stormed the U.K.'s Sizewell power plant, scaling the reactor without resistance. The goal was simply to expose the plant's vulnerability, but if the intruders had been actual terrorists the result would have been catastrophic. Finally, nuclear materials have also been known to disappear, and not just in Russia; early this year, the Japanese government admitted that it could not account for 206 kilograms of plutonium—enough to make 30 to 40 bombs.

Leaking acid waste ate through six inches of carbon steel inside the reactor of a nuclear plant in Ohio.

With the threat of climate change upon us, it is obviously that we need to move away from fossil fuels. But we also need to follow the example of Germany and reject the nuclear option in favor of renewable resources like wind and solar power. Germany only began a serious transition to renewables 10 years ago but is now the leading global producer of wind power. This industry has been an economic and ecological boon, generating clean and cheap energy and 40,000 jobs (compared to 38,000 in the entire German nuclear industry, which still produces six times the energy that wind energy does). And wind turbines and solar panels, which are decentralized and inert, make poor terrorist targets. If we are to secure our future, we must secure current stores of nuclear materials as well as ensure that we don't produce any more of them.

Analyze the essay:

1. Proponents of nuclear power have called it a "clean" energy source since it does not produce air pollution in the way that burning coal or oil does. In the article you just read, however, Assadourian describes nuclear power as a pollutant because it leaves behind radioactive nuclear waste. Would you consider nuclear power to be a clean energy source or a pollutant? Why or why not?

2. In his condemnation of nuclear power as an energy source, Assadourian claims that nuclear power presents severe security issues. In the previous viewpoint, authors Peter W. Huber and Mark P. Mills argue that nuclear power can be easily secured. After reading both essays, do you believe that security issues should be taken into account when deciding whether to use nuclear power? What pieces of evidence helped you form your opinion?

Alternative Vehicles Should Replace Gasoline-Powered Cars

Terry Backer

Terry Backer is a Connecticut representative and chair of the Connecticut House Energy and Technology Committee. In the following essay Representative Backer argues that vehicles powered by hydrogen fuel cells can be cleaner, cheaper, and more efficient than gasoline-powered vehicles. Moreover, using a homegrown source of energy can extricate America from complex political struggles abroad. He urges Americans to take initiative and pursue technologies and infrastructure that will result in the widespread use of alternatively powered vehicles.

Consider the following questions:

1. Who is Sir William Robert Grove, according to Backer?
2. According to the author, what waste products do hydrogen fuel cells emit?
3. Why does the author mention vinyl records and CD players?

Five-dollar-a-gallon gasoline. It's no stretch of the imagination anymore. In fact, it's just shy of becoming a reality. . . .

The demand for energy is growing worldwide at a rate not anticipated 20 years ago. Supplies of deeper, more difficult to reach reservoirs of oil are more costly to extract. If we learned anything from our high school economics

Terry Backer, "Freedom from Fossil Fuels," *State Legislatures*, vol. 31, February 2005. Copyright © 2005 by the National Conference of State Legislatures. Reproduced by permission.

class it is the rule of supply and demand. A greater demand coupled with a lower supply results in higher costs. Suppy is contracting worldwide (or the cost of obtaining that supply is increasing). Demand is growing at unprecedented rates in Asia and elsewhere. That equals higher prices for all of us at the pump and the light switch. Not to mention all our goods and services. . . .

We Must Replace Gasoline-Powered Automobiles

It is the automobile that we must address if we are to find energy independency for our nation.

Hydrogen fuel cell powered vehicles are where the future lies. Hydrogen is the most plentiful element on the planet. It is found in every glass of water, in natu-

English scientist William Robert Grove invented the fuel cell in the 1830s.

ral gas and even in landfill gas-sewage. This is not new technology. Sir William Robert Grove invented the fuel cell in the 1830s. Grove knew that by using electricity he could split water into hydrogen and oxygen. He theorized if you reversed the process and combined hydrogen and oxygen you would get electricity. He tried it. It worked. It still works today and after billions of dollars in investment and research, fuel cell buses and vehicles are on the road. Even more advanced models of fuel cell powered vehicles using the hybrid energy recovery systems like that used on the Honda Insight hybrid are being developed by automakers and companies like Connecticut's own United Technologies Company.

Hydrogen Is Clean and Efficient

Sir William wasn't concerned about any number of other pluses that hydrogen fuel cells also bring to the table. They are more efficient users of fuel because nothing is being burned. The waste products from the process are water and heat; two by-products that can be used again. Fuel cells are almost nonpolluting, the supply is abundant on earth and when made from water, opposed to natural gas, the energy source is renewable.

It does take energy to make hydrogen. There is no free lunch. It takes about the same amount of energy used to refine oil into gasoline and heating fuels. When using natural gas, which has lots of hydrogen in it, fuel cells work just fine. The fuel cells can't really be called renewable sources of energy when used with natural gas, but it is a bridge fuel to hydrogen generation. The cells, when used with natural gas, are far more efficient in fuel-to-energy conversion than gasoline or other combustion engines and they can be called Green, very Green.

Hydrogen Highways

Automobile manufacturers have developed fuel cell/hydrogen vehicles, and a few are already in use. But the technology can't be expanded until we start producing hydrogen fuel.

We face a chicken and egg situation when it comes to implementing fuel cell technology for our cars and trucks. The auto industry says there are no fueling stations to make the huge investment in setting up mass production and no one will build them because there are no mass manufacturing of fuel cell cars. Remember vinyl records? When the compact disc hit the market it was expected to take 15 years to penetrate because no one had CD players. Well, they just made the players and the CDs at the same time and records went the way of the Edsel [a car sold in the 1950s].

Hydrogen Cars Are the Future

Automobiles with hydrogen cells would be power stations on wheels.

Jeremy Rifkin, "Hydrogen: Empowering the People," *Nation*, December 23, 2002.

Governor Arnold Schwarzenegger is breaking some eggs in California. He has proposed the world's first hydrogen highways.

He is involving business, nonprofit groups and technical experts in developing the blueprint. A map of the routes and technical requirements was due the first of [2005]. The plan calls for a public/private partnership to create and fund the system. Funding is expected to include

This zero-emissions taxi in London is powered by a hydrogen fuel cell on the passenger side of the car.

a combination of revenue bonds, general fund appropriations and private money.

Fueling stations will be built along California's vast highway system as a public investment. Schwarzenegger is taking the first giant leap to make our energy revolution happen. . . .

We Must Invest in the Future

Fuel cells and some other alternatives are currently more expensive than the old oil driven machines, hence the reluctance to build the foundation. In a short time the world competition for oil will drive prices even higher and fuel cells will become competitive and in short order cheaper than oil. We need to build the infrastructure now

An electric car recharges its battery at a fueling station. Electric cars offer one nonpolluting alternative to gasoline-powered vehicles.

"Seems like an appropriate license plate for a SUV . . ."

Beattie. © 2001 by the *Daytona Beach News-Journal*. Reproduced by permission.

so industry can do its magic. We need to do as California is doing. Our energy flank is wide open to world market oil cost that can damage our economy and each of our pocketbooks.

Energy independence is freedom from foreign countries, their entanglements and multinational oil companies that don't really care about our country. In fact, the energy revolution may be the most patriotic thing we can do for our nation. As the founders of this country did 200 plus years ago we must now do as well— separate ourselves from foreign lords. Energy independence can be achieved. It will require public investment and putting the people's future first. We just need to be willing to invest in a future that is right around the corner. . . .

On the automotive front, hydrogen is clearly the future. It is best suited in the near term for more populated and heavily traveled regions. Governments are going to have to make a big investment in pipelines, technology and fueling stations just like we put government money behind our highway system, ports and airports. It will take time. In the interim, using ethanol and other homegrown fuels is in the best interest of our country.

Analyze the essay:

1. Representative Terry Backer acknowledges that it will take a good deal of money to jump-start a hydrogen transportation system, but he believes such an endeavor is worth pursuing. In the following essay author Brock Yates balks at the amount of money needed to make hydrogen fuel cells viable and concludes that this money is not well spent on such a project. In your opinion, should large sums of money be invested in changing America's transportation infrastructure? What are the upsides of such a change? The downsides?

2. In his essay Representative Backer compares the current energy crisis to the founding of the United States of America. What similarities does Backer see between the two events? Do you think this is a valid comparison? Why or why not?

Alternative Vehicles Are Not as Practical as Gasoline-Powered Cars

Brock Yates

Brock Yates is a writer and editor for *Car and Driver* magazine. In the following viewpoint he argues that alternative vehicles will not replace the traditional gasoline-powered automobile. He says innovations such as the electric car, the fuel-cell engine, or the transportation device known as the Segway are too inefficient, expensive, and impractical to compete with the inexpensive, convenient, and increasingly environmentally friendly gasoline-powered automobile. He cautions Americans not to waste their money on such inventions and predicts that transportation will be dependent on fossil fuels for the foreseeable future.

Consider the following questions:

1. According to the author, what are two problems that render the Segway an impractical transportation device?
2. What are three reasons Yates gives for why electric cars do not make good alternative vehicles?
3. According to the author, what effect have modern computer systems and good design had on the gasoline-powered automobile?

Bad news for the car haters. . . . The most recent great white hope to run the gas-swilling, pollution-puffing, body-shredding, four-wheeled nightmare called the automobile off the American landscape has hit a ditch.

Brock Yates, "Segway to Nowhere," *The American Spectator*, December/January 2003–2004. Copyright © 2003 by *The American Spectator*. Reproduced by permission.

The "Human Transporter" Is a Flop

You may recall the whoops of delight issuing from the elite media at [the] news that design guru Dean Kamen had solved the twenty-first-century transportation problem with his invention of "Ginger," the code-name for his revolutionary two-wheeled miracle called the Segway.

It is a computer-controlled, all-electric "Human Transporter" that resembles a power lawn mower devoid of blades and a leaf bag. Thanks to Kamen's "Dynamic Stabilization" system the Segway is capable of toddling a rider at speeds up to 15 mph while a network of microchips and tiny motors keeps the device automatically in balance. . . .

Forget that its price tag is between $4,000 and $6,000 and that operating range is limited to 6–10 miles. Enthusiasts also choose to ignore the harsh reality that the Segway hates curbs, potholes and other simple obstructions. This has prompted several ugly tumbles, including one by an Atlanta police officer after he failed to navigate a downtown curb properly.

The alternative personal vehicle known as the Segway has met with several problems that make it unfit for widespread use.

"We recommend parking every few hours to let the little guys rest."

Maass. © 2005 by Mike Maass and Lauri S. Friedman. Reproduced by permission.

Worse yet, after several hours of operation, the Segway's batteries become sufficiently drained of power that its tiny computer brains gasp for juice. . . .

Rather than a crazed rush to buy these magical devices celebrated by the ABTA (Anything But the Automobile), sales have been less than spectacular. The price tag has no doubt contributed to the limited volume of 6,000 units.

Alternative Vehicles Are Impractical

No matter, Kamen and his goofy scooter are still celebrated as a viable alternative to the hated car. . . . [Car-haters] of course choose to ignore the problems presented by, say,

100 million Segways plying the highways of the nation. Imagine the resulting overload on the wheezing power grid. This serves as another reminder that for all the sensational ideas about alternative transportation devices like electric cars, fuel-cell vehicles, mass-transit trains and buses, etc., there is a smokestack at the point of origin.

For example, while the electric car has been abandoned for a multitude of reasons—excessive weight, low performance, slow battery recharge time, expense, lead-acid, battery disposal issues—the primary cause was the realization that the national power grid could not supply sufficient juice for an electronic fleet sucking up the already limited energy supply. . . .

Some fabulists now claim the fuel-cell is the hope of the future. Most automakers are hard at work on research to

The Toyota Matrix, a fuel-efficient, combination SUV and sports car, is among the latest innovations in automobile technology.

create these magical power sources that convert Hydrogen and Oxygen into electricity and a harmless exhaust of water droplets. Nirvana! Clean energy with no downside, But a few caveats remain. One: the expense and complexity of building, much less mass-producing, the polymer-electrolyte membrane that combines Hydrogen and Oxygen to generate electricity has not been solved. Two: Hydrogen, while abundant in nature, cannot be captured cheaply without massive power inputs. Its refinement, distribution and storage (remember the *Hindenburg*) offer massive challenges that have not yet been solved. Therefore the possibility of the fuel-cell becoming a viable powerplant for normal, reasonably-priced automobiles lays far in the future, if ever—unless that revolutionary breakthrough in technology comes out of left field.

Alternative Vehicles Still Depend on Traditional Fuels

In the short term the so-called hybrid engine—a simple combination of a conventional internal-combustion engine powering a small electrical generator that in turn propels the vehicle—seems viable. Both Honda and Toyota have efficient hybrids (perhaps sold as loss-leaders) on the road, with every major automaker soon to follow.

Yet, for all the glories heaped on the hybrid as a saver of petroleum (about a 20 percent increase in fuel mileage in normal driving), one ugly truth haunts the Greenies. The primary power source for a Hybrid is the same old gasoline-powered engine of yore. Some units may employ high-efficiency diesels—providing certain stringent emission standards can be met—but the power source in the end is the same old Black Gold called Petroleum.

Gasoline-Powered Vehicles Are Cheap, Practical, and Clean

Not only is it cheap (and probably to become even cheaper when the Iraq supply returns to normal volumes), but gasoline exists within a highly efficient production and distribution network. In the old days internal combustion engines were the filthy sources of carbon dioxide, nitrous-oxide, and carbon monoxide, but modern computer engine management systems and better designs have radically reduced the dangerous emissions to a point where some advance gasoline engines actually emit exhausts cleaner than the ambient air.

Trust me, for all the cheerleading by some politicians, lobbyists, environmentalist loonies and their handmaidens in the elite media, the old flivver in your garage will be powered by a gasoline or diesel engine variant for the foreseeable future.

Analyze the essay:

1. Yates argues that one major downfall of alternative vehicles is their continued reliance on traditional fuel sources such as gasoline and electricity. In your opinion, how independent should alternative vehicles be from traditional fuels? Is it worth investing money and research into producing alternative vehicles if they are going to continue to run in part on gas and electricity? Why or why not?

2. In his essay Yates compares several different kinds of alternative vehicles to the traditional automobile. He deliberately uses strong descriptions of these alternative vehicles, casting them as "goofy" and "magical." In what way do these descriptions influence your opinion of alternative vehicles? Do you think this type of writing has a positive or negative effect on the author's argument?

Section Two: Model Essays and Writing Exercises

Using Compare and Contrast in the Five-Paragraph Essay

The last section of this book provided you with samples of previously published writing on energy alternatives. All are persuasive, or opinion, essays that make certain arguments about various topics relating to energy alternatives. Most of them also compare and contrast different facts and figures to make their arguments. This section will focus on writing your own compare-and-contrast essays on energy alternatives.

In terms of presenting information and making an argument, the compare-and-contrast method can be a very effective way to organize an essay. At the heart of the compare-and-contrast essay is the act of evaluating two or more issues, things, or ideas next to each other. Such side-by-side glances can often reveal aspects of one subject that might have gone unnoticed had it been evaluated by itself.

There are two basic ways to structure your compare-and-contrast essay. You can either evaluate your subjects point by point, analyzing them together throughout the essay. Or, you can evaluate your subjects separately, reserving the first half of the essay for one subject and the second half of the essay for the other. Sometimes you may find it is effective to mix these two approaches, but, in general, the form you choose will determine the overall structure, pacing, and flow of the essay.

Sometimes, the compare-and-contrast essay can focus on either the similarities *or* the differences between your subjects. A comparison essay usually explores the similarities between two subjects, whereas a contrast essay focuses on their differences. You can solely compare your subjects in order to present their commonality. Or, you can solely contrast your subjects in order to expose their fundamental differences. Of course, you can also compare and contrast in the same essay. This approach is useful when your subjects are not entirely similar or different, which is often the case. This method can be effective when attempting to define, analyze, or arrive at a more in-depth understanding of your subjects.

Although compare-and-contrast essays can be used to conduct objective, unbiased discussions, they are frequently useful for making persuasive arguments in which you are attempting to convince the reader of something. This effect can be achieved by presenting two subjects, either evaluating their advantages and disadvantages, or showing in what ways one is superior to another, and then advocating a course of action or expressing a preference for one over the other.

Regardless of what style of compare-and-contrast essay you choose, there are certain features common to all of them. For example, all compare-and-contrast essays focus on at least two subjects. Furthermore, all compare-and-contrast essays feature certain transitional words that signal that a similarity or difference is being pointed out (see box).

In the following section you will read some model essays on energy alternatives that use compare-and-contrast arguments, and you will complete exercises that will help you write your own. To help you, this preface will identify the main components of five-paragraph essays (as well as longer pieces) and discuss how these components fit together. It also will examine the different types of compare-and-contrast essays and how they are organized.

Components of the Five-Paragraph Essay

An essay is a short piece of writing that discusses or analyzes one topic. Five-paragraph essays are a common form of essay frequently used in school assignments and on tests such as the SAT. Every five-paragraph essay begins with an introduction, ends with a conclusion, and features three supporting paragraphs in the middle.

The introduction presents the essay's topic and thesis statement. The topic is the issue or subject discussed in the essay. All the essays in this book are about the same topic—energy alternatives. The thesis or thesis statement is the argument or main point that the essay is trying to make about the topic. The essays in this book all have different thesis statements because their arguments about energy alternatives differ.

Transitions Often Found in Compare-and-Contrast Essays

additionally	in comparison
also; too	in contrast
alternatively	in the same way
as well as	likewise
conversely	moreover
equally	on the contrary
from this perspective	on the other hand
furthermore	similarly
however	then again

The thesis statement should clearly identify for readers the main thrust of the essay. A focused thesis statement helps determine what the core of the essay is about; the subsequent paragraphs develop and support its argument.

In addition to presenting the thesis statement, a well-written introductory paragraph captures the attention of the reader and explains why the topic being explored is important. It may provide the reader with background information on the subject matter or feature an anecdote that illustrates a point relevant to the topic. It could also present startling information that clarifies the point of the essay or a contradictory position that the essay will refute. Further techniques for writing an introduction are found later in this section.

The introduction is then followed by three (or more) supporting paragraphs. These are the main body of the essay. The writer can use various kinds of material to back up the topics of each supporting paragraph. These may include statistics, descriptive details, quotations from people with special knowledge or expertise, historic facts or past events, and anecdotes. A rule of good writing is that specific and concrete examples are more convincing than vague, general, or unsupported assertions.

The conclusion is the paragraph that closes the essay. Also called the ending or summary paragraph, its function is to summarize or reiterate the main idea of the essay. It may recall an idea from the introduction or briefly examine the larger implications of the thesis. Because the conclusion is also the last chance a writer has to make an impression on the reader, it is important that it not simply repeat what has been presented elsewhere in the essay but rather close it in a clear, final, and memorable way.

Pitfalls to Avoid

When writing five-paragraph essays, there are a few common pitfalls to avoid. Most of the writing you do should be written in the third person; unless you are writing a narrative piece or a memoir, it is usually inappropriate to use "I" when writing. Express your ideas without saying "I think" or "I believe." Instead, use phrases such as "It seems likely . . ." or "It should be pursued because . . ." to express the idea you support without getting personally involved in the essay. Using a removed, objective third-person writing voice will help your essay sound authoritative and professional.

When writing essays about controversial issues such as energy alternatives, it is important to remember that disputes over the material are common precisely because there are many different perspectives from which to evaluate your subjects. Because it is likely that your subjects will be not all good or all bad, it is important to state your arguments in careful and measured terms. Evaluate your subjects fairly—avoid overstating negative qualities of one subject or understating positive qualities of another. Extreme words such as *always* or *never* posit an absolute stance on an issue without exception. Try instead to use words that qualify the argument, such as *most likely, most often,* or *rarely.* When one position does end up being stronger than another, make sure you show this through examples, facts, and details instead of absolute statements.

Another pitfall to avoid when writing compare-and-contrast essays is to attempt to study two subjects that are not comparable or contrastable. For example, you could write a simple compare-and-contrast essay that focuses on the similarities and differences of oranges and apples or T-shirts and sweaters. You would not, however, want to set out to compare oranges and tables or T-shirts and rice. The subjects you choose to compare or contrast must be linked in a basic way so that they warrant an examination. In terms of energy alternatives, it makes sense to compare and contrast nuclear power with renewable resources because they are both forms of power. It would not, however, make sense to compare nuclear power to the manufacturing of cars because they are inherently different subjects.

Fossil Fuels: A Greater Threat

Editor's Notes A compare-and-contrast essay can be written in several ways. One way is to describe thing A, describe thing B, and then compare them. The following five-paragraph essay compares fossil fuels and renewable resources in this style. It examines the environmental impact of each energy source and then explains why one does greater harm than the other. Each paragraph contains supporting details and information, some of which were taken from the viewpoints found in Section One of this book. The essay then concludes with a paragraph that restates the essay's main idea—that while both fossil fuels and renewable resources affect the environment, fossil fuels pose a greater risk to the planet's health.

As you read this essay, take note of its components and how it is organized. In addition, consider the following questions:

1. How does the introduction engage the reader's attention?
2. What kinds of supporting evidence are used to back up the essay's arguments?
3. What purpose do the essay's quotes serve?
4. How does the author transition from one idea to another?

The first sentence establishes the topic of the essay—energy sources.

Nearly all aspects of modern society depend on an energy source. Energy fuels the cars, buses, trains, and planes that get people from place to place, and it powers the appliances and devices that run in homes and businesses. It takes energy to grow food and to manufacture products. Much of this energy comes from fossil fuels such as oil, coal, or natural gas. Other portions of it come from renewable resources, such as wind and solar power. Although fossil fuels can generate large quantities of valuable energy, they often produce by-products that pollute the air and water. On the other hand, renewable resources do not emit pollution, but their necessary infrastructures can take up large amounts of space, encroaching on habitat and harming wildlife. While both types of energy sources leave a footprint on the planet, fossil fuels wreak more serious harm on the environment than do renewable resources. In order to understand how, it is necessary to compare and contrast the main ways in which fossil fuels and renewable resources affect the environment.

The phrase "on the other hand" indicates a comparison is being made.

This is the thesis statement for the paragraph and the essay.

Fossil fuels damage the environment by causing air and water pollution and by contributing to global environmental problems. Exhaust from gasoline-powered cars causes smog, especially in heavily populated cities such as Los Angeles and New York City. Extracting oil and natural gas from deep in the ocean sometimes results in oil spills that kill wildlife and make land and sea uninhabitable. The most serious consequence of using fossil fuels for energy is their contribution to the phenomenon known as global warming. When fossil fuels are burned, they produce gases such as carbon dioxide that collect in the earth's atmosphere. When too much of these gases are present, they trap heat in the atmosphere, causing the planet to warm. Over time, these slight increases in temperature can have disastrous environmental consequences. Ice caps can melt and cause sea levels to rise, which in turn threaten to flood low-lying islands, erode shores, and destroy marine life. Furthermore, experts contend global warming can cause an increase in disease; trigger severe weather such as tornados, earthquakes, and hurricanes; and threaten the normal growth of food crops. Although there is much debate over what the exact nature of global warming might be over time, it is clear that fossil-fuel consumption is altering the planet's normal systems.

This is the thesis statement of the second paragraph.

Supporting details and specific examples are provided.

Specific examples are provided so the reader has a thorough understanding of what the author means by "disastrous environmental consequences."

Says earth scientist Wallace S. Broecker, who is with the Lamont-Doherty Earth Observatory in New York, "To take a chance and say these abrupt changes won't occur in the future is sheer madness."[1]

Renewable resources, on the other hand, negatively affect the environment in different yet significant ways. In order to generate wind or solar power, large machines known as wind turbines or solar photovoltaic panels must be erected to harness wind or sunlight. These machines can threaten natural habitat. In fact, generating enough electricity to power the United States would require covering more than 9 million acres with turbines and panels, an area about the size of Connecticut, Delaware, and Massachusetts put together. Such an event would have drastic consequences for wildlife. In addition to losing precious territory and mating grounds, birds and small animals can be killed if they get caught up in the giant turbine blades, and the turbines themselves can disrupt migratory patterns. As the editors of the *Colorado Springs Gazette* have asked, "How many thousands of acres of beloved 'open space' are windmill farm backers willing to obliterate along the way? . . . How much endangered species habitat consumed? . . . And how many fluffy little mountain plovers [a type of bird] are we willing to sacrifice annually to those whirling turbine blades?"[2] Clearly, using wind and solar power can carry environmental consequences.

Although neither fossil fuels nor renewable resources are completely environmentally harmless, fossil fuels pose a more severe threat to the overall health of the earth. While it is unfortunate that wind turbines and solar panels threaten birds and other wildlife, global warming threatens the survival of everyone on the planet and is thus a more significant environmental threat. Further-

1. Quoted in John Carey, "Global Warming: Consensus Is Growing Among Scientists, Governments, and Business That They Must Act Fast to Combat Climate Change," Rainforest Action Network, www.ran.org, August 6, 2004.
2. *Colorado Springs Gazette*, "Tilting at Windmills; City Energy Policy Shouldn't Be Duped by the Romance of 'Renewables,'" October 25, 2003.

more, the burning of fossil fuels produces air pollution, which is a health threat to not only birds and other wildlife but also to humans. Indeed, according to the Natural Resources Defense Council, air pollution kills more than sixty-four thousand Americans every year and sickens thousands more. In addition, the extraction risks associated with fossil fuels do not exist for renewable resources. Although they may damage habitat, no toxic chemicals or life-threatening substances are associated with harnessing wind or solar power.

It is often said that when it comes to energy, there is no "free lunch"—that is, there is no way to power modern society without affecting the environment in some way. Given this reality, we should seek power sources that have the least environmental impact possible. Whereas both types of energy sources have an impact on the health of the environment, the burning of fossil fuels is more dangerous to the planet's health than the erection of solar panels and wind turbines.

> The author's conclusion is based on the comparisons that were made throughout the essay.

Exercise One
Create an Outline from an Existing Essay

It often helps to create an outline of the five-paragraph essay before you write it. The outline can help you organize the information, arguments, and evidence you have gathered from your research.

For this exercise, create an outline that could have been used to write Essay One: "Fossil Fuels: A Greater Damage." This "reverse engineering" exercise is meant to help familiarize you with how outlines can help classify and arrange information.

To do this you will need to articulate the essay's thesis, identify important pieces of evidence, and point out key comparisons that support the argument. Part of the outline has already been filled in to give you an idea of the assignment.

Outline

Write the essay's thesis:

I. Paragraph 2: Fossil fuels damage the environment by causing air and water pollution and by contributing to global environmental problems.

    a. The damaging effects of retrieving fossil fuels from the earth

        i. Oil spills can be hazardous

    b. Produces carbon dioxide, which contributes to global warming

        i.

        ii. Could trigger disease, cause severe weather, and affect crop growth

II. Paragraph 3:

    a.

    b. Can injure or kill wildlife

III. Paragraph 4:

    a.

    b.

    c. Wind and solar power do not emit toxic chemicals.

Alternative Vehicles Are Preferable to Gasoline-Powered Cars

Editor's Notes The second essay, also written in five paragraphs, is a slightly different type of compare-and-contrast essay than the first model essay. In the first essay, the author examined two different subjects separately and then compared their differences and expressed a preference for one. In the following essay, the author uses the entire essay to express a preference for one thing over another and has organized each paragraph to compare a different element of the subject.

The following essay presents three different reasons why the author believes alternatively powered vehicles are superior to gasoline-powered ones. As in the first essay, these supporting paragraphs use some material from the viewpoints presented in Section One of this book.

The notes in the sidebars provide questions that will help you analyze how this essay is organized and how it is written.

It is often said that Americans have an ongoing love affair with their automobiles. The average American puts about seventeen thousand miles on his or her vehicle every year, and cars are used to transport more people to their homes and businesses than any other kind of vehicle. Clearly, America is a driving society. But are Americans driving smart? The overwhelming majority of the vehicles driven in the United States run on gasoline, which is derived from fossil fuels. But gasoline-powered cars pollute the environment, have looming costs, and hold grave political consequences. These are just some of the reasons why alternatively powered vehicles should replace gasoline-powered cars, and the sooner the better.

How does the introduction help frame the essay and introduce the topic?

Where in this paragraph is the essay's thesis statement found?

Where is the topic sentence for this paragraph? What supporting details are used?

What does the Rifkin quote add to the argument?

What transitions are used in the paragraph?

How does the first sentence help transition between paragraph one and paragraph two?

What sources are cited to support the topic? Are they effective?

What comparisons are being made in this paragraph?

What transitions do you see? What purpose do they serve?

One main reason why alternative vehicles should be pursued is because they are more environmentally friendly than traditional gasoline-powered vehicles. For example, the by-products of one type of alternative engine, the hydrogen fuel cell, are just water and heat, two nonpolluting products that can be reused. Conversely, gasoline-powered engines emit pollution that releases greenhouse gases into the atmosphere, which contributes to global warming, a potentially dangerous weather trend that could have drastic consequences for the planet. Hydrogen expert Jeremy Rifkin says that changing to hydrogen would "dramatically reduce carbon dioxide emissions and mitigate the effects of global warming."[1] Furthermore, pollution from gasoline-powered vehicles stands to rise in the near future. As more countries switch to industrial economies that are fossil-fuel based, pollution will increase.

The growing consumption of oil reveals another reason to pursue alternative vehicles. As the world's fossil fuel reserves are exhausted, the dwindling supply becomes more valuable and difficult to reach, and thus more expensive. As author Thom Hartmann explains, "When about half the oil has been removed from an underground oil field, it starts to get much harder (and thus more expensive) to extract the remaining half. The last third to quarter can be excruciatingly expensive to extract."[2] Therefore, as the oil supply dwindles, it will become increasingly expensive to drive a gasoline-powered vehicle. Alternative vehicles could offer a more economical mode of transportation. Furthermore, gasoline-powered vehicles tend to get low mileage, which burns more gas and costs even more. In comparison, alternatively powered vehicles tend to go much farther on much less; as a result, they are much more affordable to operate. The cost-effective choice is the alternatively powered vehicle.

1. Jeremy Rifkin, "Hydrogen: Empowering the People," *Nation*, December 23, 2002.
2. Thom Hartmann, "The End of Ancient Sunlight," *Yes!* Fall 2004.

Finally, alternative vehicles are preferable to gasoline-powered ones because they have the potential to extricate the United States from complicated, expensive, and dangerous international conflicts. Most of the oil the United States uses comes from other places in the world. In fact, the United States consumes about 25 percent of the world's oil, yet it sits atop just 3 percent of its supply. Much of this imported oil comes from places such as the Middle East. But the Middle East is a notoriously unstable and volatile area—as journalist Tim Appenzeller puts it, "The Middle East remains the mother lode of crude, but war and instability underscore the perils of depending on that region."[3] The United States itself has gotten involved in several wars in order to, among other reasons, ensure easy access to cheap oil. Such situations endanger the lives of American soldiers and cost the country billions of dollars. In comparison, alternatively powered vehicles are free from such entanglements. Hydrogen, ethanol, wind, solar, and even nuclear power, all of which could provide fuel for alternative vehicles, can be manufactured at home. If the United States no longer needed to import vast quantities of fossil fuels, it could avoid having to protect its oil supply abroad.

It is unlikely that Americans will give up their taste for driving or abandon their need to move rapidly around the country. Therefore, it makes environmental, economic, and political sense to replace the traditional gasoline-powered automobile with alternatively powered vehicles. Our skies, oceans, and rivers will thank us. We can save money and avoid being at the mercy of international oil cartels. And we can help preserve a peaceful world order by avoiding conflict over natural resources. When deciding between alternatively powered vehicles and gasoline-powered ones, the choice of the future is clear.

Where is the topic sentence for the fourth paragraph?

What are some of the supporting details of this paragraph?

How does the author return to the ideas presented in the introduction?

How does the writer avoid simply repeating the main ideas of the essay?

3. Tim Appenzeller, "The End of Cheap Oil," *National Geographic*, June 2004.

Create an Outline for an Opposing Compare-and-Contrast Essay

For this exercise, your assignment is to find supporting ideas, create an outline, and ultimately write a compare-and-contrast essay that argues a view that opposes that of the second model essay. Using information from Section One of this book and your own research, you will write an essay that supports the following thesis statement: Improving gasoline-powered cars is better than developing alternatively powered vehicles.

Part 1: Brainstorm and Collect Information

Before you begin writing, you will need to think carefully about what ideas your essay will contain. Coming up with these ideas is a process known as brainstorming. Brainstorming involves jotting down any and all ideas that might make good material when you finally begin to write.

Begin the brainstorming process by asking yourself a few questions. In what ways are traditional automobiles superior to alternative vehicles? What further advantages might they have over alternative vehicles if they were to be improved upon? Use outside research or the material in Section One to come up with at least three arguments. Each argument should illustrate a clear reason why gasoline-powered cars, if improved upon, could be superior to alternative vehicles.

For each of the ideas you come up with, write down facts or information that support it, again drawing from the viewpoints in the previous section and in the appendices. These could be:

- statistical information,
- direct quotations from the articles,
- anecdotes of past events,
- and/or comparative information that clearly shows how one thing is superior to another.

As an example, consider this paragraph topic: Traditional cars are more economical than alternative vehicles. The following list illustrates the types of supporting material that would be useful in writing this paragraph.

- Alternative vehicles such as the Segway cost between four and six thousand dollars and can be unreliable, impractical, and dangerous.
- According to energy expert Robert L. Bradley Jr., world supplies of oil are estimated to last about 114 years. Probable world supplies of natural gas are estimated to last about 200 years, and the world's probable supply of coal will last about 1,884 years. These numbers indicate that the earth is not short on fossil fuels; thus, it is unlikely that gasoline will become dramatically more expensive.
- Alternative energy sources can be very expensive to use. Brock Yates writes in Viewpoint Eight: "Hydrogen, while abundant in nature, cannot be captured cheaply without massive power inputs." Likewise, cars can run on ethanol, a biomass fuel derived from corn, but planting, growing, and harvesting enough corn to make sufficient amounts of ethanol is a difficult and expensive endeavor.
- Gasoline-powered vehicles already have an extensive infrastructure in place. Brock Yates writes in Viewpoint Eight: "Not only is it cheap . . . but gasoline exists within a highly efficient production and distribution network." Comparatively, it will be enormously expensive to create the infrastructure to support alternative vehicles, such as the hydrogen highways proposed in California.

Sometimes you can develop ideas by critically examining the claims your opponent makes. For example, the model essay claims that alternative vehicles are more environmentally friendly than gasoline-powered cars. Is this necessarily true? Remember from Viewpoint Eight in Section

One that author Brock Yates claims that state-of-the-art technology is making gasoline-powered automobiles burn more cleanly than ever. Learn to retain information like this that could potentially be used to argue against a particular claim.

Part 2: Place the Information from Part 1 in Outline Form

Thesis statement: Improving gasoline-powered cars is better than developing alternatively powered vehicles.

    I. Reason A

        i. details and elaboration

    II. Reason B

        i. details and elaboration

    III. Reason C

        i. details and elaboration

Part 3: Write the Arguments in Paragraph Form

You now have three arguments that support the paragraph's thesis statement as well as supporting material. Use the outline to write your three supporting arguments in paragraph form. Make sure each paragraph has a topic sentence that states the paragraph's thesis clearly and broadly. Then, add supporting sentences that use the facts, quotes, and examples that support the paragraph's argument. The paragraph may also have a concluding, or summary, sentence.

Exercise Three

Using Quotations to Enliven Your Essay

No essay is complete without quotations. Quotations can serve many functions when used properly in an essay: They can present statistics, deliver anecdotes, express first-person testimony, and provide expert advice. Get in the habit of using quotes to support at least some of the ideas in your essays. Quotes do not need to appear in every paragraph, but they do need to appear often so that the essay contains voices aside from your own. When you write, use quotations to accomplish the following:

- offer expert opinion to lend authority to an argument,
- cite lively or passionate passages that express emotional or firsthand accounts,
- include a particularly well-written point that gets to the heart of the matter,
- and supply statistics or facts that have been derived from someone's research.

There are a few important things to remember when using quotations. If you are using direct quotations or statements of other people, it is a good idea to note their qualifications and biases. This way your reader can identify the person you have quoted and can put his or her words into context. Also, be sure to clearly put any quoted material within proper quotation marks. Failing to attribute quotes to their authors constitutes plagiarism, which is when an author takes someone else's words or ideas and presents them as his or her own. Plagiarism is a very serious infraction and must be avoided at all costs. For more information on using quotations, consult Appendix B.

Assignment 1: Reread the essays presented in Sections One and Two of this book and find at least one example of each of the above quotation types.

Examining Nuclear Power and Renewable Resources

Editor's Notes Sometimes the compare-and-contrast essay can expose your readers to information and then let them draw their own conclusions. The following compare-and-contrast essay demonstrates such a style by highlighting the similarities and differences between two types of energy sources. Unlike the previous model essays, however, this essay does not attempt to make a persuasive argument. It compares and contrasts nuclear power with solar and wind power, but it does not take a position on which power source should be pursued or which is an overall better energy source.

This essay also differs from the previous model essays in that it is longer than five paragraphs. Sometimes five paragraphs are simply not enough to adequately develop an idea. Extending the length of an essay can allow the reader to explore a topic in more depth or can present multiple pieces of evidence that together provide a more complete picture of a topic.

As you read, consider the questions posed in the margins. Continue to identify thesis statements, supporting details, transitions, and quotations. Examine the introductory and concluding paragraphs to understand how they shape the essay. Finally, evaluate the essay's general structure and assess its overall effectiveness.

What technique does the author use to introduce the essay?

The autumn of 1973 marked a dramatic turning point in the world's relationship with its most widely used energy source, oil. In October of that year, political events in the Middle East led the Organization of Petroleum Exporting Countries (OPEC) cartel, the main producer of oil in the world, to block oil sales to the United States. Over the next five months, the United States experienced an unprecedented energy crisis. Drivers waited in long lines to buy gasoline, which was doled out on alternating days based on license plate numbers and completely banned from sale on Sundays. Although the embargo was lifted in March 1974, the crisis underscored the United States's dependency on oil for economic survival and its need to incorporate alternative sources of energy into its economy. Three energy sources—nuclear power, wind power, and solar power—are frequently hailed as being viable energy alternatives that could replace or supplement fossil fuels. A close comparison of these three alternative energy sources reveals that they have some similarities but, on the whole, are very different sources of power.

What is the essay's thesis statement?

One important feature shared by nuclear, wind, and solar power is that they are each capable of being produced in America, thereby offering the United States much-needed energy independence. Nuclear power plants can be constructed on American soil; already there are 103 operational nuclear power plants around the country. Furthermore, the fuel for these plants—uranium—can also be harvested at a variety of deposits in North America. Like nuclear power plants, solar panels can be constructed in the vast expanses of desert around the country or even on the rooftops of individual homes and businesses in especially sunny states. Similarly, wind turbines can stretch the length of America's spacious plains and also be erected offshore, as has been done off the coasts of several European nations, including Denmark, Sweden, and the United Kingdom. All three types of power can help the United States develop a domestic energy economy that would extricate it from complicated, costly, and dangerous international situations that are necessary to secure access to oil.

What kinds of details serve to support the paragraph's thesis?

Nuclear, wind, and solar power are also similar in that they are all potentially affordable sources of power. Nuclear power can cost just ten to fourteen cents per kilowatt-hour, and small amounts can go far. Peter W. Huber and Mark P. Mills, experts on energy and power, write, "An ounce of enriched-uranium fuel equals about 4 tons of coal, or 15 barrels of oil. That's why minuscule quantities contained in relatively tiny reactors can power a metropolis."[1] In addition, the technologies that make wind and solar power possible continue to become more affordable; in some parts of the country, solar power costs twenty to twenty-five cents per kilowatt-hour, and wind power costs as little as four to six cents per kilowatt-hour. In contrast, places such as California charge up to thirty-five cents per kilowatt-hour for traditional energy during peak times. Furthermore, the cost of traditional utilities, which derive their power from fossil fuels, are rising—they went up 6 percent in 2003, making power generated by renewable resources an even better deal.

Despite these commonalities, nuclear, wind, and solar power also have many significant differences. One of the greatest differences between them is that solar and wind power are renewable resources, but nuclear power is an exhaustible resource. Solar and wind power are "renewable" because they come from endless sources of energy—that is, it is impossible to run out of sunlight or wind. In contrast, nuclear power is generated from the element uranium, which must be mined from the ground. Although the earth is endowed with many deposits of uranium ore, there is still a finite amount of uranium on the planet. Therefore, like fossil fuels, nuclear power depends on a natural resource that cannot be replaced once it is used up.

Another important distinction between nuclear, wind, and solar power is that they each require a very different kind of space. Nuclear power plants can generate massive amounts of power while occupying a very small amount of space. As energy experts Huber and Mills write: "The stunning thing about nuclear power [is that]

What kinds of transitions are used to switch from one idea to another?

How is the essay shifting its focus?

What kinds of authorities are quoted throughout the essay?

1. Peter W. Huber and Mark P. Mills, "Why the U.S. Needs More Nuclear Power," *City Journal*, Winter 2005.

tiny quantities can do so much. A bundle of enriched-uranium fuel-rods that could fit into a two-bedroom apartment in Hell's Kitchen [a neighborhood in New York] would power the city for a year."[2]

On the other hand, solar panels and wind turbines require large areas in order to generate worthwhile quantities of power. Tens of thousands of acres of desert habitat would need to be paved in order to make room for the number of solar panels that could effectively capture light and convert it to usable energy. Such construction would gobble up animal habitat and threaten the survival of many species, yet produce comparatively small amounts of power. The editors of the *Colorado Springs Gazette* newspaper ask, "Will wind farms any time soon be able to supplant a traditional power plant in delivering the most energy bang for the buck? That's unlikely, unless advocates intend that we pave all of eastern El Paso County with windmills and solar panels."[3]

How does the author make the transition from one paragraph to another smooth and fluid?

Although renewable resources take up large amounts of space, they have one very critical advantage over nuclear power: They are less vulnerable to terrorist attack. Indeed, nuclear power plants are considered by many to be an ideal terrorist target. If blown up, they could cause horrific damage on a nearly incomprehensible scale—exactly the kind of destruction that terrorists seek to unleash. In January 2003 the activist group Greenpeace staged a mock terrorist attack on a British nuclear power plant to show just how vulnerable it was. The activists were able to access the nuclear reactor without any problem; if the attack had been real, it could have had disastrous consequences.

On the contrary, renewable resources tend not to invite terrorism because they do not contain explosive materials. Likewise, they are often spread out in remote areas or clustered on personal property. As reporter Erik

2. Huber and Mills, "Why the U.S. Needs More Nuclear Power."
3. *Colorado Springs Gazette*, "Tilting at Windmills; City Energy Policy Shouldn't Be Duped by the Romance of 'Renewables,'" October 25, 2003.

Assadourian puts it, "Wind turbines and solar panels, which are decentralized and inert, make poor terrorist targets."[4] Therefore, nuclear power and renewable resources have very different kinds of safety concerns.

Yet another difference between nuclear, wind, and solar power involves the waste products they leave behind. Although they are all "clean" energy sources in the sense that none of them produce air pollution or contribute to global warming, nuclear power produces nuclear waste, which can stay toxic for millennia. It is so toxic, in fact, that it can eat through the very vats that are meant to contain it for hundreds of thousands of years. Nuclear reactors also release radioactive waste into the environment. The air, soil, and groundwater of nearby areas become polluted, threatening the health of local populations. Environmental activist Deborah Katz has described the effect that two nuclear reactors have had on her community:

What does first-person testimony bring to the essay?

> We have an epidemic of disease, including statistical significance in breast cancer, non-Hodgkin's Lymphoma and Multiple Myeloma, a rare blood cancer. We have a tenfold increase in children with Down Syndrome, high rates of learning disabled and handicapped children, and high rates of immune deficiency and auto immune diseases.[5]

Wind and solar power, in contrast, have no harmful by-products. For example, author David Case says that if the United States switched to wind power, there would be "no nuclear waste, no emissions, no pollution of any kind. Fewer children would choke on smog. Every year, wind could spare thousands of lives that would otherwise be cut short from lung disease."[6]

In 1973, the American people were first confronted with the consequences of being entirely dependent on

4. Erik Assadourian, "The New Clear Threat," *Worldwatch*, May/June 2003.
5. Deborah Katz, "Nuclear Power Threatens Communities," *Resist*, November 2004.
6. David Case, "Cleaner than Cows," www.tompaine.com, June 4, 2001.

oil, and so they began to seek alternatives to an oil-based economy. These alternative sources share some features, but, on the whole, nuclear, wind, and solar power are very different sources of power. Together they offer some important advantages over fossil-fuel use, such as decreased costs and providing the United States with a domestically based fuel economy. However, space, efficiency, safety concerns, and by-product emissions are just a few of the many differences among them. Both their commonalities and their differences should be taken into account when considering alternatives to fossil fuels.

Does the conclusion return to the main point of the essay introduced in the first paragraph?

Exercise Four

Examining Introductions and Conclusions

Every essay features introductory and concluding paragraphs that are used to frame the main ideas presented. Along with presenting the essay's thesis statement, well-written introductions should grab the attention of the reader and make clear why the topic being explored is important. The conclusion reiterates the essay's thesis and is also the last chance for the writer to make an impression on the reader. Strong introductions and conclusions can greatly enhance an essay's effect on an audience.

The Introduction
There are several techniques that can be used to craft an introductory paragraph. An essay can start with:
- an anecdote: a brief story that illustrates a point relevant to the topic.
- startling information: true and pertinent facts or statistics that elucidate the point of the essay.
- setting up and knocking down a position: a position or claim believed by proponents of one side of a controversy, followed by statements that challenge that claim.

- historical perspective: an example of the way things used to be that leads into a discussion of how or why things work differently now.
- summary information: general introductory information about the topic that feeds into the essay's thesis statement.

Remember, in a compare-and-contrast essay, the introductory paragraph should clearly establish what subjects are being examined. If it is a persuasive essay in which the writer is comparing two subjects and then advocating one over another, this, too, should be made clear in the introduction.

Assignment 1: Reread the introductory paragraphs of the model essays and of the eight viewpoints in Section One. Identify which of the techniques described above are used in the viewpoints. How do they grab the attention of the reader? Are their thesis statements clearly presented?

Assignment 2: Write an introduction for the essay you have outlined and partially written from Exercise Two. You can use one of the techniques described above.

The Conclusion

The conclusion brings the essay to a close by summarizing or returning to its main ideas. Good conclusions, however, go beyond simply repeating these ideas. Strong conclusions explore a topic's broader implications and reiterate why it is important to consider. They may frame the essay by returning to an anecdote featured in the opening paragraph. Or, they may close with a quotation or refer back to an event in the essay. In opinionated essays, the conclusion can reiterate which side the essay is taking or ask the reader to reconsider a previously held position on the subject.

Assignment 3: Reread the concluding paragraphs of the model essays and of the eight viewpoints in Section One. Which were most effective in driving their arguments home to the reader? What sorts of techniques did they use to do this? Did they appeal emotionally to the reader or bookend an idea or event referenced elsewhere in the essay?

Assignment 4: Write a conclusion for the essay you have outlined and partially written in Exercise Two. Try using one of the techniques described above.

Assignment 5: Review the five-paragraph essay you have written. Make sure it has a clear introduction that draws the reader in and contains a thesis statement that concisely expresses what your essay is about. Evaluate the paragraphs and make sure they each have clear topic sentences that are well supported by interesting and relevant details. Check that you have used compelling and authoritative quotes to enliven the essay. Finally, be sure you have a solid conclusion that uses one of the techniques presented in this exercise.

Exercise Five

Writing a Compare-and-Contrast Five-Paragraph Essay

The final exercise is to write your own five-paragraph compare-and-contrast essay that deals with the topic of energy alternatives. You can use the resources in this book for information about energy alternatives and how to structure a compare-and-contrast essay.

The following steps are suggestions on how to get started.

Step 1: Choose Your Topic

Think carefully before choosing the topic for your compare-and-contrast essay. Is there any subject that particularly fascinates you? Is there an issue you strongly support or strongly oppose? Is there a topic you would like to learn more about? Ask yourself such questions before selecting your essay topic. See Section Three: Supporting Research Material for possible paper topics or come up with your own paper topic idea.

Step 2: Write Down Questions and Answers About the Topic

Recall from Exercise Two the process known as brainstorming, in which you ask yourself questions and come up with ideas to discuss in your essay. Possible questions that will help you with the brainstorming process include the following:

- Why is this topic important?
- Why should people be interested in this topic?
- How can I make this essay interesting to the reader?
- Do I want to write an informative essay or an opinionated essay?
- What question am I going to address in this paragraph or essay?
- What facts, ideas, or quotes can I use to support the answer to my question?
- Will the question's answer reveal a preference for one subject over another?

Questions especially for compare-and-contrast essays include:

- Have I chosen subjects that I can compare or contrast?
- What characteristics do my subjects share?
- What is different about my subjects?
- Is one subject consistently superior to another?
- Is one subject consistently inferior to another?

Step 3: Gather Facts and Ideas Related to Your Topic

This book contains several places to find information, including the viewpoints and the appendices. In addition, you may want to research the books, articles, and Web sites listed in Section Three or do additional research in your local library.

Step 4: Develop a Workable Thesis Statement

Use what you have written down in steps two and three to help you articulate the main point or argument you want to make in your essay.

For example, consider the following two possible thesis statements:

- Gasoline-powered automobiles, not cars powered by hydrogen fuel cells, are the vehicles of the future. (This could be the thesis statement of an opinionated compare-and-contrast essay that examines why gasoline-powered cars are superior to cars powered by hydrogen fuel cells.)
- Fossil fuels and nuclear power share many similarities, but they also have stark differences that mark them as unique types of power. (This could be the thesis statement of a nonpersuasive compare-and-contrast essay that explores the similarities and differences of two subjects but stops short of expressing a preference for one over the other.)

Step 5: Write an Outline or Diagram

1. Write the thesis statement at the top of the outline.
2. Write roman numerals I, II, and III on the left side of the page.
3. Next to each roman numeral, write down the best arguments or ideas you came up with in Step 3. These should all directly relate to and support the thesis statement. If the essay is solely a compare or solely a contrast essay, write down three similarities or three differences between your subjects. If it is a persuasive compare-and-contrast essay, write down three reasons why one subject is superior to the other.
4. Next to each letter write down facts or information that support that particular idea.

An alternative to the roman numeral outline is a diagram.

Diagrams: Alternative to Outlines

Some students might prefer to organize their ideas without using the roman numeral outline. One way to do this is to use the diagram method. Compare-and-contrast essays are especially well suited for the diagram method, which allows you to physically visualize the similarities and differences between your subjects. A possible approach would be as follows:

1. Draw two intersecting circles in the middle of a page so that one side of each overlaps.
2. On the left side of the page above the first circle, write "Subject A." In this circle, write all of the things that are unique to one subject.
3. On the right side of the page above the second circle, write "Subject B." Use this circle to jot down all of the things that are unique to the other subject.
4. In the middle of the page, above where the two circles intersect, write "A and B." In this intersected space, write all of the things that are common to both subjects.

Step 6: Write the Three Supporting Paragraphs

Use your outline to write the three supporting paragraphs. Write down the main idea of each paragraph in sentence form. Do the same thing for the supporting points of information. Each sentence should support the paragraph of the topic. Be sure you have relevant and interesting details, facts, and quotes (see Exercise Three for information on using quotes). Use transitions when you move from idea to idea to keep the text fluid and smooth. Sometimes, although not always, paragraphs can include a concluding or summary sentence that restates the paragraph's argument.

Step 7: Write the Introduction and Conclusion

See Exercise Four for information on writing introductions and conclusions.

Step 8: Read and Rewrite

As you read, check your essay for the following:

- Does the essay maintain a consistent tone?
- Do all sentences serve to reinforce your general thesis or your paragraph theses?
- Do all paragraphs flow from one to the other? Do you need transition words or phrases?
- Have you quoted from reliable, authoritative, and interesting sources?
- Is there a sense of progression throughout the essay? Does each paragraph advance the argument by offering more information than the preceding paragraphs?
- Does the essay get bogged down in too much detail or irrelevant material?
- Does your introduction grab the reader's attention? Does your conclusion refer back to any previously discussed material? Does it give the essay a sense of closure?
- Are there any spelling or grammatical errors?

Tips on Writing Effective Compare-and-Contrast Essays

- You do not need to describe every possible similarity or difference of your subjects. Focus on the most important ones that support your thesis statement.
- Write in the active, not passive, voice.
- Vary your sentence structure, especially when stating and restating your thesis.
- Maintain a professional, objective tone of voice. Avoid sounding uncertain or insulting.
- Anticipate what the reader's counterarguments may be and answer them.
- Use sources that state facts and evidence.
- Do not write in the first person.
- Avoid assumptions or generalizations without evidence.
- Aim for clear, fluid, well-written sentences that together compose an essay that is informative, interesting, and memorable.

Section Three: Supporting Research Material

Facts About Energy Alternatives

Editor's Note: These facts can be used in reports or papers to reinforce or add credibility when making important points or claims.

Oil Around the World

- Humans have extracted about 742 billion barrels of oil from the earth.
- According to the U.S. Geological Survey, between 1.4 trillion and 2.1 trillion barrels of oil are left in the ground. At current consumption rates, this amount would last between 63 and 95 years.
- About 82 million barrels of oil are used worldwide each day. About 30 billion barrels are used every year, a figure that constantly grows as more countries become industrialized.
- According to the U.S. National Intelligence Council, 80 percent of the world's oil and 95 percent of its natural gas have yet to be extracted from the earth.
- Sixty-five percent of the world's oil reserves are found in the Middle East.
- In 2005 oil prices fetched record highs of more than fifty dollars per barrel.

Oil and the United States

- The United States has about 4.7 percent of the world's population, yet it consumes about 25 percent of the world's energy.
- The United States is responsible for producing 25 percent of the world's carbon dioxide pollution from fossil-fuel consumption.
- Two-thirds of America's oil consumption is used for transportation needs.
- Each American consumes an average of three gallons of gasoline per day.

- The United States possesses just 3 percent of the world's oil reserves.
- According to the U.S. Department of Energy, by 2020 the United States is expected to import more than 70 percent of its oil.

Fossil Fuels and Pollution

- Every year more than 6 billion tons of carbon dioxide are released into the atmosphere from fossil-fuel consumption. Carbon dioxide traps heat in the earth's atmosphere and contributes to global warming.
- According to the Natural Resources Defense Council, air pollution kills more than sixty-four thousand Americans every year and sickens thousands more.
- To extract coal from the earth, mountaintops are moved or blown off, watersheds are filled with tailings, and toxic ponds of a substance known as slurry are left behind.

Renewable Resources

- In the 1980s a kilowatt-hour from solar energy cost around $2.50. Today, solar power costs between 20 and 25 cents per kilowatt-hour.
- According to the book *Renewable Energy Sources for Fuels and Electricity*, the United States receives more energy from forty minutes of sunlight than from the energy it burns from fossil fuels in an entire year.
- According to the Union of Concerned Scientists, one hundred square miles in the Nevada desert could produce enough solar electricity to power the entire country.
- Power generated from renewable resources can be intermittent; it can be very difficult and expensive to store energy for use at night, on cloudy or windless days, and during peak usage hours.
- According to Paul K. Driessen of the nonprofit public policy energy group the Center for the Defense of Free Enterprise, one thousand acres of solar panels produces as much electricity as a gas-fired generator that takes

up two to five acres. It takes four thousand acres of wind turbines to generate an equivalent amount of power.

- In 2002 wind farms provided electricity for 40 million Europeans.
- The European Wind Energy Association estimates that by 2020 wind will satisfy the electricity needs of 195 million people—half the population of western Europe.
- It would take an estimated 260 to 300 square miles of wind turbines to generate the amount of power produced by one nuclear plant.
- Because they can be a danger to migrating birds, the Sierra Club has referred to wind turbines as "Cuisinarts of the air." American scientists estimate that wind turbines near San Francisco have killed as many as forty-four thousand birds since the 1980s.
- According to the U.S. Department of Energy, if the wind in North Dakota and South Dakota could be adequately harvested, it could meet two-thirds of America's electricity needs.
- By 2030 the United States plans to supply 10 percent of its energy needs with hydrogen.
- A study produced by the World Wildlife Fund claimed that the development of renewable energy resources could result in 700,000 new jobs by 2012 and 1.3 million new jobs by 2020.

Automobiles

- The average American drives about 8,964 miles per year.
- According to *OnEarth* magazine, Americans drive 60 percent more total miles than German, French, British, Japanese, Canadian, Mexican, and Swedish drivers combined.
- By 2020 1.1 billion automobiles are expected to be on the world's roads. India alone is expected to add 14 million vehicles by then.
- The average gasoline-powered vehicle is parked 96 percent of the time.

- Automobiles have a wide range of how many miles they get to a gallon of gasoline. The Toyota Prius, a hybrid gasoline-electric car, gets around fifty-five miles per gallon. In comparison, the SUV Hummer 2 gets between eight and eleven miles per gallon.

Nuclear Power

- Lithuania gets 80 percent of its electricity from nuclear power. France derives 78 percent of its electricity from nuclear power, and Slovakia gets 57 percent of its electricity from nuclear power. The United States relies on nuclear power for about 20 percent of its energy needs.
- A single kilogram of uranium undergoing various stages of nuclear fission, the process that turns it into power, can ultimately produce 7 million kilowatt-hours of power.
- A 1991 report by the National Cancer Institute concluded that there is "no general increased risk of death from cancer for people living in 197 U.S. counties containing or closely adjacent to 62 nuclear facilities."
- When uranium is mined, radioactive tailings are left behind. The U.S. government has spent more than $1.5 billion cleaning up such refuse from mines in Utah and New Mexico.
- Radioactive waste from nuclear reactors must be stored for at least three hundred thousand years.
- Nuclear power plants provide electricity to one in every five American homes and businesses.
- More than thirty-seven American power plants have failed mock security drills since 1995.
- According to *Science World* magazine, one pound of nuclear fuel generates fifty-two megawatt-hours of electricity, enough energy to power every home in Detroit for an entire week.
- Scientists believe that the air, soil, and water in the Chernobyl area will be toxic for up to three hundred years.

Finding and Using Sources of Information

When you write a compare-and-contrast essay, or any kind of essay, it is necessary to find information to support your point of view. You can use sources such as books, magazine articles, newspaper articles, and online articles.

Using books and articles

You can find books and articles in a library by using the library's cataloging system. If you are not sure how to use these resources, ask a librarian to help you. You can also use a computer to find many magazine articles and other articles written specifically for the Internet.

You are likely to find a lot more information than you can possibly use in your essay, so your first task is to narrow it down to what is likely to be most usable. Look at book and article titles. Look at book chapter titles and examine the book's index to see if it contains information on the specific topic you want to write about.

For a five-paragraph essay, you do not need a great deal of supporting information, so quickly try to narrow down your materials to a few good books and magazine or Internet articles. You do not need dozens. You might even find that one or two good books or articles contain all the information you need.

You probably do not have time to read an entire book, so find the chapters or sections that relate to your topic, and skim these. When you find useful information, copy it onto a notecard or notebook. You should look for supporting facts, statistics, quotations, and examples.

Evaluate the Source

When you select your supporting information, it is important that you evaluate its source. This is especially important with information you find on the Internet.

Because nearly anyone can put information on the Internet, there is as much bad information as good information. Before using Internet information—or any information—try to determine whether the source seems to be reliable. Is the author or Internet site sponsored by a legitimate organization? Is it from a government source? Does the author have any special knowledge or training relating to the topic you are looking up? Does the article give any indication of where its information comes from?

Using Your Supporting Information

When you use supporting information from a book, article, interview or other source, there are three important things to remember:

1. Make it clear whether you are using a direct quotation or a paraphrase. If you copy information directly from your source, you are quoting it. You must put quotation marks around the information and tell where the information comes from. If you put the information in your own words, you are paraphrasing it.

Here is an example of using a quotation:
> David Case argues that using renewable resources could have far-reaching political benefits for the United States. Says Case: "Imagine an energy supply free of oil tankers, the *Exxon Valdez*, and war in the Persian Gulf. No OPEC tyrants to befriend, no business . . . human rights atrocities in the name of cheap energy."[1]

Here is an example of a brief paraphrase of the same passage:
> David Case urges people to consider how America could benefit from being freed from dependence on fossil fuels. The United States would no longer have to negotiate with corrupt businessmen, support cruel dictators, or fight wars in order to secure access to affordable oil.

1. David Case, "Cleaner than Cows," www.tompaine.com, June 4, 2001.

2. Use the information fairly. Be careful to use supporting information in the way the author intended it. For example, it is unfair to quote an author as saying, "Nuclear power works" when he or she intended to say, "Nuclear power works *against the people's best interests.*" This is called taking information out of context. This is using supporting evidence unfairly.
3. Give credit where credit is due. You must give credit when you use someone else's information, but not every piece of supporting information needs a credit.
   - If the supporting information is general knowledge—that is, it can be found in many sources—you do not have to cite (give credit to) your source.
   - If you directly quote a source, you must give credit.
   - If you paraphrase information from a specific source, you must give credit.

If you do not give credit where you should, you are *plagiarizing*—or stealing someone else's work.

Your teacher will probably want you to give credit in one of three ways:
1. Informal: As in the examples in number 1 above, you tell where you got the information in the same place you use it.
2. Informal list: At the end of the article, place an unnumbered list of the sources you used. This tells the reader where, in general, you got your information.
3. Formal: Use a footnote, like the first example in number 1 above. (A footnote is generally placed at the end of an article or essay, although it may be located in different places depending on your teacher's requirements.)

Be sure you know exactly what information your teacher requires before you start looking for your supporting information so that you know what information to include with your notes.

Sample Essay Topics

Compare-and-Contrast Essays

Compare and Contrast Solar Power with Wind Power

Compare and Contrast Nuclear Power with Fossil Fuels

Nuclear Energy Pollutes More than Fossil Fuels

Fossil Fuels Pollute More than Nuclear Power

Nuclear Power Is a More Powerful Energy Source than Solar or Wind Power

Renewable Resources Are Better for the Environment than Nuclear Power

Fossil Fuels Cause More Damage to the Environment than Renewable Resources

Renewable Resources Damage the Environment as Badly as Fossil Fuels Do

Renewable Resources Are More Expensive than Nuclear Power or Fossil Fuels

Fossil Fuels Cost More than Nuclear Power or Renewable Resources

Alternatively Powered Vehicles Are Superior to Gasoline-Powered Vehicles

Alternatively Powered Vehicles Will Not Replace Gasoline-Powered Vehicles

General Persuasive Topics

The World Is Running Out of Oil

The World Is Not Running Out of Oil

America Should Drill for Oil in Wildlife Reserves

America Should Not Drill for Oil in Wildlife Reserves

America's Dependence on Foreign Oil Makes It Vulnerable to Terrorism

Nuclear Power Plants Are Safe from Terrorist Attack

Nuclear Power Plants Are Vulnerable to Terrorism

Energy Conservation Is the Best Way to Solve the Energy Crisis

Conserving Energy Is Not a Long-Term Solution to the Energy Crisis

Fossil Fuel Consumption Destroys the Environment

Damage Caused by Fossil Fuel Consumption Is Exaggerated

Automobiles Cause Air Pollution

Air Pollution from Automobiles Has Been Reduced

Extracting Oil Damages the Environment

Oil Companies Aim to Protect the Environment While Drilling

Nuclear Waste Is Safely Containable

Nuclear Waste Is Dangerous to People's Health

Organizations to Contact

American Petroleum Institute (API)
1220 L St. NW, Washington, DC 20005
(202) 682-8000 • Web site: www.api.org

The American Petroleum Institute represents America's petroleum industry. Its activities include lobbying, conducting research, and setting technical standards for the petroleum industry.

American Solar Energy Society (ASES)
2400 Central Ave., Suite G-1, Boulder, CO 80301
(303) 443-3130 • e-mail: ases@ases.org
Web site: www.ases.org

The ASES promotes solar energy. It disseminates information on solar energy to schools, universities, and the community. In addition to the *ASES Publications Catalog*, the society publishes the bimonthly magazine *Solar Today*.

American Wind Energy Association (AWEA)
122 C St. NW, Suite 380, Washington, DC 20001
(202) 383-2500 • e-mail: windmail@awea.org
Web site: www.awea.org

The American Wind Energy Association promotes wind energy as a clean source of electricity for consumers around the world.

Council on Alternative Fuels (CAF)
1225 I St. NW, Suite 320, Washington, DC 20005
(202) 898-0711

The CAF comprises companies interested in the production of synthetic fuels and the research and development of synthetic fuel technology. It publishes information on new alternative fuels in the monthly publication *Alternate Fuel News*.

Energy Conservation Coalition (ECC)
1525 New Hampshire Ave. NW, Washington, DC 20036
(202) 745-4874

The ECC is a group of public interest organizations that promote energy sufficiency. It supports government policies that encourage energy conservation.

Environmental Protection Agency (EPA)
Ariel Rios Bldg., 1200 Pennsylvania Ave. NW
Washington, DC 20460
(202) 272-0167 • Web site: www.epa.gov

The EPA is the federal agency in charge of protecting the environment and controlling pollution. The agency works toward these goals by enacting and enforcing regulations, identifying and fining polluters, assisting businesses and local environmental agencies, and cleaning up polluted sites.

Foundation for Clean Air Progress (FCAP)
1801 K St. NW, Suite 1000L, Washington, DC 20036
(800) 272-1604
e-mail: info@cleanairprogress.org
Web site: www.cleanairprogress.org

The FCAP is a nonprofit organization that believes the public is unaware of the progress that has been made in reducing air pollution. The foundation represents various sectors of business and industry in providing information to the public about improving air quality trends.

International Association for Hydrogen Energy (IAHE)
PO Box 248266, Coral Gables, FL 33124
(305) 284-4666 • Web site: www.iahe.org

The IAHE is a group of scientists and engineers involved with the production and use of hydrogen for energy. It sponsors international forums to further its goal of creating an energy system based on hydrogen.

National Biodiesel Board (NBB)
3337A Emerald Ln., PO Box 104898
Jefferson City, MO 65110
(573) 635-3893 • e-mail: info@biodiesel.org
Web site: www.biodiesel.org

The National Biodiesel Board is a national trade association representing the biodiesel industry. Its membership includes state, national, and international feedstock and feedstock processor organizations, biodiesel suppliers, fuel marketers and distributors, and technology providers.

National Renewable Energy Laboratory (NREL)
1617 Cole Blvd., Golden, CO 80401-3393
(303) 275-3000 • Web site: www.nrel.gov

The National Renewable Energy Laboratory is the U.S. Department of Energy's laboratory for renewable energy research. Some of the areas of investigation at the NREL include wind energy, biomass-derived fuels, advanced vehicles, solar manufacturing, hydrogen fuel cells, and waste-to-energy technologies.

Nuclear Energy Institute (NEI)
1776 I St. NW, Suite 400, Washington, DC 20006-3708
(202) 739-8000 • e-mail: webmasterp@nei.org
Web site: www.nei.org

The Nuclear Energy Institute is the policy making organization of the nuclear energy industry, and its objective is to promote policies that benefit the nuclear energy business. NEI has more than 260 members in fifteen countries.

Pew Center on Global Climate Change
2101 Wilson Blvd., Suite 550, Arlington, VA 22201
(703) 516-4146 • Web site: www.pewclimate.org

The Pew Center on Global Climate Change is a nonpartisan organization dedicated to educating the public and policy makers about the causes and potential consequences of global climate change and informing them of ways to reduce the emissions of greenhouse gases.

Bibliography

Books

Paula Berinstein, *Alternative Energy: Facts, Statistics, and Issues.* Westport, CT: Oryx, 2001.

Daniel D. Chiras, *The Natural House: A Complete Guide to Healthy, Energy-Efficient, Environmental Homes.* New York: Chelsea Green, 2000.

Kenneth S. Deffeyes, *Beyond Oil: The View from Hubbert's Peak.* New York: Farrar, Straus and Giroux, 2005.

Rex A. Ewing, *Power with Nature: Solar and Wind Energy Demystified.* Masonville, CO: PixyJack, 2003.

David Goodstein, *Out of Gas: The End of the Age of Oil.* New York: W.W. Norton, 2004.

Peter Hoffman, *Tomorrow's Energy: Hydrogen, Fuel Cells, and the Prospects for a Cleaner Planet.* Cambridge, MA: MIT Press, 2001.

Peter W. Huber and Mark P. Mills, *The Bottomless Well: The Twilight of Fuel, the Virtue of Waste, and Why We Will Never Run Out of Energy.* New York: Basic Books, 2005.

Robert C. Morris, *The Environmental Case for Nuclear Power: Economic, Medical, and Political.* St. Paul, MN: Paragon House, 2000.

Joseph J. Romm, *The Hype About Hydrogen: Fact and Fiction in the Race to Save the Climate.* Washington, DC: Island, 2004.

Vijay V. Vaitheeswaran, *Power to the People: How the Coming Energy Revolution Will Transform an Industry, Change Our Lives, and Maybe Even Save the Planet.* New York: Farrar, Straus and Giroux, 2003.

Periodicals

Lester R. Brown, "The Short Path to Oil Independence: Together, Hybrid Cars and Wind Farms Can Slash Our Oil Imports," *Mother Earth News*, February/March 2005.

H. Sterling Burnett, "Wind Power Puffery," *Washington Times*, February 4, 2004.

Joe F. Colvin, "Nuclear Power Plants Are Vital for Energy, Diversity, Clean Air," *Electric Light & Power*, September 2003.

Julie Creswell, "Oil Without End?" *Fortune*, February 17, 2003.

Thom Hartmann, "The End of Ancient Sunlight," *Yes!* Fall 2004.

Denis Hayes and Lisa A. Hayes, "Oil and Power: Never Have the Weaknesses Caused by America's Dependence on Fossil Fuels Been More Apparent. And Never Have the Alternatives Looked So Good," *OnEarth*, Winter 2002.

Albert L. Huebner, "The Cost of Fossil Fuels," *Humanist*, March/April 2003.

Marianne Lavelle, "Living Without Oil," *U.S. News & World Report*, February 17, 2003.

David Morris, "A Hydrogen Economy Is a Bad Idea," February 24, 2003, www.alternet.org/envirohealth/15239.

Gordon Prather, "Nuclear Energy; Not Exactly What the Greens Had in Mind," *Washington Times*, September 4, 2002.

Wendy Priesnitz, "Solar in the City," *Natural Life*, November/December 2004.

Andrew Simms, "It's Time to Plug in the Renewable Power: Fossil Fuels Not Only Wreck the Climate, They Also Keep the World Poor," *New Scientist*, July 3, 2004.

Walter Simpson, "We Must Do More with Less—the Case for Conservation Saving Energy: Does It Make Sense?" *Buffalo (NY) News*, July 29, 2001.

Brandon Spun, "Clearing the Air of Nuclear Myths," *Insight on the News*, May 20, 2002.

Caitlin Thomas and Burke Franklin, "Drilling in the Arctic National Wildlife Refuge," *Wildlife Society Bulletin*, Summer 2002.

Index

Picture Credits

About the Editor

Lauri S. Friedman earned her bachelor's degree in religion and political science from Vassar College. Much of her studies there focused on political Islam, and she produced a thesis on the Islamic Revolution in Iran titled "Neither West, Nor East, But Islam." She also holds a preparatory degree in flute performance from the Manhattan School of Music and is pursuing a master's degree in history at San Diego State University. She has edited over ten books for Greenhaven Press, including *At Issue: What Motivates Suicide Bombers?*, *At Issue: How Should the United States Treat Prisoners in the War on Terror?*, and *Introducing Issues with Opposing Viewpoints: Terrorism*. She currently lives near the beach in San Diego with her yellow lab, Trucker.